Low Carb Recipes Fast & Easy!

by
Belinda Schweinhart

with
Chaddie Letson

Brass Pig, LLC

The information in this book is based upon the latest data made available by government agencies, food manufacturers and trade associations. The data contained herein is the most complete and accurate information available as this book goes to press. It is important to note that all nutrient breakdowns for processed foods are subject to change by, and are different between, manufacturers without notice and therefore may vary from printing to printing.

ISBN 0-9671821-3-1

Printed in the United States of America.

First Edition	May, 1999	ISBN 0-9671821-0-7
Second Edition	March, 2001	ISBN 0-9671821-2-3
Third Edition	February, 2003	

Published by

Brass Pig, LLC
PO Box 43091
Louisville, KY 40253
1-888-229-9677

www.LowCarbRecipes.com

www.LowCarbCookbooks.com

Table of Contents

Introduction

This book contains real, great tasting, easy recipes. They are all low carb, no sugar, no flour recipes suitable for anyone following the Atkins diet, the Protein Power Plan, the Carbohydrate Addicts Diet, the Zone and the Neanderthin diet as well as those needing no sugar recipes for diabetic diets. When was the last time you ate a really good cookie without feeling guilty? Try the peanut butter cookie on page 147.

I know there are hundreds, if not thousands, of low carb recipes on the Internet. I've personally tried many of them. The problem I've found is that 1) they don't taste very good and I'm not wasting any of my carbs on something that is marginal, 2) the carb counts frequently aren't right and 3) they are too complicated.

(Note – All carb counts used in this cookbook have been obtained from the USDA Internet data base. See page 12 for address.)

I owned and operated a restaurant for six years to a daily packed house crowd and am well aware of pleasing the customer, repeatability and ease of a recipe, the need to be specific with ingredient brands and just plain eye appeal. I spent a lot of time doing up front developing on a recipe so it could be prepared by <u>anyone</u> from the instructions on the wall.

My best advise for anyone wanting to follow a low carb diet is to get the book of the plan you are going to follow and read the book – all of it. There are a lot of self-proclaimed experts due to their experiences, but nothing can replace getting the facts from the real experts. Again, read the books.

Check our companion web site for all the latest low carb books and cookbooks at **www.LowCarbCookbooks.com** .

Belinda Schweinhart

About the Authors . . .

Belinda Schweinhart started the Atkins diet in January, 1998, after trying every other diet available. None worked, at least not for very long. She knew diabetes and low blood sugar were prevalent in her family. After 6 months, she had lost 40 pounds, and more importantly, gone from size XXL to size MEDIUM! Cholesterol went from 251 (with HDL of 54 – test didn't show other numbers, darn it!), to 234 (with HDL of 61, LDL of 140 and tryglycerides of 165) after only six months, and had cholesterol of 225 (with HDL of 64, LDL of 126 and tryglycerides of 174) after one year. *After two years of following the low carb diet, her cholesterol is now only 184 (with HDL of 65, LDL of 96 and triglycerides of 114).* Her tests are better with every test.

It has been 36 months and she has continued to keep the weight off and still feels great eating low carb!

Chaddie Letson found her way to the low carb way of thinking because of her husband's onset of adult diabetes. Her husband's doctor suggested that he consider the low carb diet. After 3 months on the diet, he lost 40 pounds, lowered his bad cholesterol (LDL) by 30 points and increased his good cholesterol (HDL) by 20 points. But the most remarkable result was that he was able to go off his diabetes medicine . . . his blood sugar went from 356 to 146!

We love this way of eating! We can no longer call this a "diet."

What can I buy at the grocery?

Five Brothers® Alfredo or Alfredo Mushroom Sauce
    2 grams carbs per ¼ cup (0 g fiber)

Five Brothers® Tomato Alfredo Sauce
    7 grams carbs per ¼ cup (1 g fiber)

Ragu® Double Cheddar or 4 Cheese Alfredo or Light Parmesan Alfredo Pasta Sauce
    2 grams carbs per ¼ cup (0 g fiber)

Ragu® Roasted Garlic Parmesan or Classic Alfredo Pasta Sauce
    3 grams carbs per ¼ cup (0 g fiber)

Healthy Choice® Mushroom Alfredo or 4 Cheese Alfredo Sauce
    3 grams carbs per ¼ cup (0 g fiber)

Newman's Own® Pasta Sauce – several flavors
    9 grams carbs per ½ cup (3 g fiber)

Breakstone's® Sour Cream
    1 gram carbs per 2 TBSP. (0 g fiber)

Frigo® Cheese Heads String Cheese
    less than 1 gram carbs per piece (0 g fiber)

Kraft® Deluxe American Cheese Slices *(not cheese food)*
    less than 1 gram carbs per slice (0 g fiber)

Parmesan Cheese – grated
    .2 grams carbs per 1 TBSP. (0 g fiber)

Kraft® Shredded Parmesan Cheese
    1 gram carbs per 1/3 cup (0 fiber)

Frigo® Ricotta Cheese, skim
    2 grams carbs per ¼ cup (0 g fiber)

Cottage Cheese, 4% small curd only
    2 grams carbs per ½ cup (0 g fiber)

Kraft® Philadelphia Cream Cheese
.8 grams carbs per 1 ounce (6.4 grams per 8 ounces) (0 g fiber)

Half & Half (cream)
.6 grams carbs per 1 TBSP. (10.4 grams per cup) (0 g fiber)

Heavy Whipping Cream
.4 grams carbs per 1 TBSP. (6.6 grams per cup) (0 g fiber)

Reddi Wip® Whipped Light Cream *(contains sugar)*
less than 1 gram carbs per 2 TBSP. (0 g fiber)

Healthy Life® 100% Whole Wheat Bread
16 grams carbs per 2 slices (6 g fiber)

Healthy Life® White Bread
16 grams carbs per 2 slices (4 g fiber)

Irene's Health Bakery® Garlic Gluten Bread
4 grams carbs per slice (0 g fiber)

Irene's Health Bakery® German Rye Bread
5 grams carbs (1 g fiber)

Jell-O® Instant Sugar-Free Pudding Mix *(contains aspertame)*
6 grams carbs per ¼ package mix (0 g fiber)
(8 grams carbs per ¼ package for chocolate mix)

Jell-O® Sugar-Free Gelatin Mix *(contains aspertame)*
1 gram carbs per ¼ package (0 g fiber)

Hillshire Farm® Beef Smoked Sausage
7 grams carbs per 14 ounce package (0 g fiber)

Swanson® Fat-Free Chicken Broth
1 gram carbs per cup (0 g fiber)

Lunchmeats, Hotdogs, etc (not Light or Fat-Free)
Various – read the labels!

Canned Chicken
0 grams carbs per ¼ cup   (0 g fiber)

Canned Tuna
0 grams carbs per ¼ cup (0 g fiber)

Pork Rinds
0 grams carbs (0 g fiber)

Rudolph's® Bacon Snaps Microwave Pork Rinds
0 grams carbs (0 g fiber)

Bacon Bits, real
0 grams carbs (0 g fiber)

Eggs, large
.6 grams carbs each (0 g fiber)

Pour-A-Quiche® Three Cheese and Broccoli & Cheddar
4 grams carbs per 1/6 pie (1 g and .5 g fiber)

Pour-A-Quiche® Spinach & Onion
7 grams carbs per 1/6 pie (.5 g fiber)

Hellmann's® Real Mayonnaise
0 grams carbs (0 g fiber)

Salad Dressings (not Lite or Fat-Free)
Various - read the labels!

Assorted Extracts
1.4 grams carbs per 1 TBSP. (0 g fiber)

Assorted Spices
Various - see page 16

Walnut pieces chopped
16.5 grams carbs per cup (8.0 g fiber)

Pecan pieces chopped
16.5 grams carbs per cup (11.4 g fiber)

Pumpkin Seed Kernels
30.5 g carbs per cup (8.9 g fiber)

Almonds
   28.0 g carbs (16.7 g fiber)

Hazelnuts
   19.2 g carbs per cup (7.3 g fiber)

Peanuts, oil roasted
   27.3 g carbs per cup (13.3 g fiber)

Peanuts, dry roasted
   31.0 g carbs per cup (11.5 g fiber)

Macadamia Nuts
   17.2 g carbs per cup (10.7 g fiber)

Planters® Dry Roasted Sunflower Kernels
   6 grams carbs per ¼ cup (4 g fiber)

Fifty 50® Peanut Butter *(no sugar added)*
   6 grams carbs per 2 TBSP. (2 g fiber)

Swiss Miss® Diet Hot Cocoa Mix *(contains Splenda®)*
   4 grams carbs per envelope (1 g fiber)

Worcestershire Sauce
   1 gram carbs per 1 tsp. (0 g fiber)

Kikkoman® Soy Sauce
   0 grams carbs (0 g fiber)

ReaLemon® Lemon Juice
   0 grams carbs per 1 tsp. (0 g fiber)

Sugar Twin® (or Brown), Splenda® or Equal® Granular Sweetener
   1 gram carbs per 2 tsp. (0 g fiber)

Sugar Twin®, Sweet 'n Low®, Equal® or Splenda® Packet Sweetener
   1 gram carbs per packet (0 g fiber)

Splenda® Tablets Sweetener
   1 gram carbs per tablet (0 g fiber)

Saco® Unsweetened Cocoa
2.6 grams carbs per 1 TBSP. (1.3 g fiber)

Hershey's® Unsweetened Cocoa
3.0 grams carbs per 1 TBSP. (1 g fiber)

Nestlé® Unsweetened Cocoa
3.0 grams carbs per 1 TBSP. (2 g fiber)

Baker's® Unsweetened Baking Chocolate
8 grams carbs per 1 ounce (4 g fiber)

Nestlé® Unsweetened Baking Chocolate
10 grams carbs per 1 ounce (6 g fiber)

Good Humor® Sugar Free Popsicle *(sweetened with aspartame)*
3 grams carbs (0 g fiber)

Good Humor® No Sugar Added Creamsicle *(sweetened with aspartame)*
5 grams carbs (0 g fiber)

Kool-Aid® or Wylers® unsweetened drink mix
0 g carbs (0 g fiber)

Kool-Aid® or Wylers® or Tang® sugar-free drink mix *(sweetened with aspartame)*
0 g carbs (0 g fiber)

Crystal Light® sugar-free drink *mix* *(sweetened with aspartame and ace-sulfame potassium)*
0 g carbs (0 g fiber)

Veryfine® Fruit2O flavored water *(sweetened with Splenda®)*
0 g carbs (0 g fiber)

Diet Ice Botanicals® flavored *water* *(sweetened with Splenda®)*
0 g carbs (0 g fiber)

What can I buy at the health food store?

Hodgson Mill® Vital Wheat Gluten
   32 grams carbs per cup (16 grams fiber)

Bob's Red Mill® Vital Wheat Gluten Flour
   6 grams carbs per 1/4 cup (0 grams fiber)

Xanthan Gum
   8 grams carbs per 1 TBSP. (9 g fiber)

Guar Gum
   6 grams carbs per 1 TBSP. (6 g fiber)

Fearn® Soya Powder
   7 grams carbs per ¼ cup (3.5 g fiber)

Unsweetened Coconut
   2 grams carbs per 3 TBSP. (1 g fiber)

Arrowhead Mills® Peanut Butter *(no sugar added)*
   6 grams carbs per 2 TBSP. (1 g fiber)

Bob's Red Mill® Flax Seed Meal
   4 grams per 2 tbsp. (4 g fiber)

NOW® Stevia Packets *(herbal sugar substitute)*
   1 gram carbs per packet (0 g fiber)

Bran-a-crisp® crackers
   6 grams carbs (2 g fiber)

Bob's Red Mill® Oat Flour
   18 grams carbs per 1/3 cup (2 g fiber)

Arrowhead Mills® Oat Flour
   20 grams carbs per 1/3 cup (4 g fiber)

Wasa Crispbread Fiber Rye
   7 grams carbs each (2 g fiber)

Soy Flour
> 9 grams carbs (6 g fiber)

Flax Seed Meal
> 4 grams carbs (4 g fiber)

Westbrae® Natural West Soy Unsweetened Soy Beverage
> 5 grams carbs per 1 cup (4 g fiber)

Sweet–n-Safe® Sweetener *(contains acesulfame potassium)*
> 1 gram carbs per packet (= 4 teaspoons sugar equivalency)

Pumpkorn®
> 4 grams carbs (2 g fiber) per 1/3 cup

Just The Cheese®
> 2 grams carbs (0 fiber) per bag

Kavli® Crispy Thin Crispbread
> 13 grams carbs (2 g fiber) per 3 pieces

Yves® Veggie Pizza Pepperoni
> 4 grams carbs (3 g fiber) per 16 slices

Westsoy® Soy Slendar Soymilk *(contains Splenda®)*
> 4 grams per 1 cup (3 g fiber)

CARB COUNTS For OTHER foods not listed :

http://www.nal.usda.gov/fnic/cgi-bin/nut_search.pl
(USDA for foods in general)

http://www.cyberdiet.com/ni/htdocs/sc_ffquest.html
(for fast foods)

http://www.stanford.edu/group/ketodiet/ketomeds.html
(for medicines)

The Complete Book of Food Counts by Corinne T. Netzer
(Dell Publishing, 1997)

Carbohydrates Calories & Fat in your food by Dr. Art Ulene (Avery
Publishing Group, 1995)

Carb counts for Assorted Flours:

Flour	Carb count
Almond Meal	18.8 carbs (11.2 fiber) / cup
Cashew Meal	44.8 carbs (4.1 fiber) / cup
Oatmeal	51.8 carbs (8.8 g fiber) / cup
Oat Flour	60.0 carbs (12.0 g fiber) / cup
Full Fat Soy Flour	29.9 carbs (8.2 g fiber) / cup
Defatted Soy Flour	38.4 carbs (17.5 g fiber) / cup
Walnut Meal	11.0 carbs (5.4 g fiber) / cup
Wheat Bran	38.8 carbs (25.7 g fiber) / cup
Wheat Germ	51.8 carbs (13.2 g fiber) / cup
Rye Flour	79.0 carbs (14.9 g fiber) / cup
Rice Bran	41.2 carbs (17.4 g fiber) / cup
Pecan Meal	63.4 carbs (13.6 fiber) / cup
Low Fat Peanut Flour	18.8 carbs (9.5 fiber) / cup
Macadamia Meal	18.4 carbs (11.2 fiber) / cup
Hazelnut Meal	12.5 carbs (7.3 fiber) / cup
Whole Wheat Flour	76.0 carbs (3.0 g fiber) / cup
All-Purpose Flour	85.0 carbs (0 fiber) / cup
Fearn® Soya Powder	28.0 carbs (14.0 g fiber) / cup
Vital Wheat Gluten	32.0 carbs (16.0 g fiber) / cup (Hodgens Mill®)
Wheat Gluten Flour	24.0 carbs (0 fiber) / cup (Bob's Red Mill®)

1 cup wheat flour =   3/4 cup soy flour
1/2 cup nut meal
1-1/3 cup oat flour
1-1/4 cup rye flour
1 cup Fearn® soya powder

2 cups wheat flour =   1-1/4 cup vital wheat gluten flour
+ 3/4 cup oat flour
+ 1/4 cup soy flour

CARB COUNTS for SPICES

1 TBSP. — USDA Nutrient Values

ALLSPICE, GROUND	4.327 g carbs (1.296 g fiber)
ANISE SEED	3.351 g carbs (0.978 g fiber)
BASIL, GROUND	2.743 g carbs (0.796 g fiber)
BAY LEAF, CRUMBLED	1.349 g carbs (0.473 g fiber)
CARAWAY SEED	3.343 g carbs (2.546 g fiber)
CARDAMOM, GROUND	3.971 g carbs (1.624 g fiber)
CELERY SEED	2.688 g carbs (0.767 g fiber)
CHERVIL, DRIED	0.933 g carbs (0.215 g fiber)
CHILI POWDER	4.099 g carbs (2.565 g fiber)
CINNAMON	5.430 g carbs (3.692 g fiber)
CLOVES, GROUND	4.040 g carbs (2.257 g fiber)
CORIANDER LEAF, DRIED	0.935 g carbs (0.187 g fiber)
CORIANDER SEED	2.749 g carbs (2.095 g fiber)
CUMIN SEED	2.654 g carbs (0.630 g fiber)
CURRY POWDER	3.663 g carbs (2.092 g fiber)
DILL SEED	3.641 g carbs (1.393 g fiber)
DILL WEED, DRIED	1.730 g carbs (0.422 g fiber)
FENNEL SEED	3.033 g carbs (2.308 g fiber)
FENUGREEK SEED	6.477 g carbs (2.731 g fiber)
GARLIC POWDER	6.108 g carbs (0.160 g fiber)
GINGER, GROUND	3.822 g carbs (0.675 g fiber)
MACE, GROUND	2.677 g carbs (1.071 g fiber)
MARJORAM, DRIED	1.029 g carbs (0.308 g fiber)
MUSTARD SEED, YELLOW	3.913 g carbs (0.739 g fiber)
NUTMEG, GROUND	3.450 g carbs (1.456 g fiber)
ONION POWDER	5.243 g carbs (0.371 g fiber)
OREGANO, GROUND	2.899 g carbs (0.675 g fiber)
PAPRIKA	3.846 g carbs (1.422 g fiber)
PARSLEY, DRIED	0.672 g carbs (0.134 g fiber)
PEPPER, BLACK	4.148 g carbs (1.696 g fiber)
PEPPER, RED OR CAYENNE	3.001 g carbs (1.325 g fiber)
PEPPER, WHITE	4.871 g carbs (1.860 g fiber)

POPPY SEED	2.085 g carbs (2.570 g fiber)
POULTRY SEASONING	2.427 g carbs (0.418 g fiber)
PUMPKIN PIE SPICE	3.880 g carbs (0.829 g fiber)
ROSEMARY, DRIED	2.114 g carbs (1.406 g fiber)
SAFFRON	1.373 g carbs (0.082 g fiber)
SAGE, GROUND	1.215 g carbs (0.360 g fiber)
SAVORY, GROUND	3.024 g carbs (2.011 g fiber)
TARRAGON, GROUND	2.411 g carbs (0.355 g fiber)
THYME, GROUND	2.749 g carbs (0.800 g fiber)
TURMERIC, GROUND	4.415 g carbs (1.435 g fiber)

OTHER

BAKING POWDER	3.822 g carbs (0.027 g fiber)
BAKING SODA	0 g carbs (0 g fiber)
CREAM OF TARTAR	5.535 g carbs (0.018 g fiber)

Where do I buy on the Internet?

Atkins Nutritionals
185 Oser Ave.
Hauppauge, NY 11788
800-6-ATKINS
888-7-ATKINS fax
www.atkinscenter.com
www.atkinsdiet.com
●Atkins foods, nutritionals

(The) Baker's Catalog
PO Box 876
Norwich, VT 05055-0876
1-800-827-6836
1-800-343-3002 fax
www.kingarthurflour.com
●flours, dough conditioners
appliances

CarbSmart
PO Box 608
Lake Forest, CA 92630
877-279-7091
949-829-9524 fax
www.carbsmart.com
●assorted foods, books,
house brands and
Nutritionals

Diet Depot
10422 Taft Street
Pembroke Pines, FL 33026
877-260-8361
954-432-2977 fax
www.dietdepot.com
●Asst. foods, nutritionals,
books

D'Lites of Shadowood
9975 Glades Road
Boca Raton, FL 33434
888-937-5262
561-488-4203 fax
www.lowcarb.com
●Asst. foods, nutritionals,
books

Platinum Nut
PO Box 325
Hughsun, CA 95326
209-883-1707
209-883-4554 fax
www.eatalmonds.com
●almonds and almond flour

Expert Foods
PO Box 1855
Ellicott City, MD 21041
www.ExpertFoods.com
●not/Sugar, not/Starch,
not/Cereal, Mousse mix,
frozen fudge bar mix,
other mixes

Global Drugs, Inc.
6448 Old Banff Coach Rd. SW
Calgary, Alberta Canada T3H2H4
403-246-1227
403-246-1228 fax
www.globaldrugs.com/
pharmacy/fsearch.htm
●Asst. sugar substitutes

GNC (General Nutrition Center)
In your neighborhood
shopping center
800-477-4462 (store locator)
www.gnc.com
●asst. bars, Designer
Protein, asst. drink mixes,
nutritionals

Ketogenics, Inc.
1330-13 Lincoln Ave.
Holbrook, NY 11741
800-943-5386
631-580-2817 fax
www.ketogenics.com
●house brand bread, muffin,
syrup mixes

La Tortilla Factory
3635 Standish Ave.
Santa Rosa, CA 95407
www.latortillafactory.com
●low carb tortillas

Lewis Brothers Bakeries, Inc.
P.O Box 6471
500 N. Fulton Ave.
Evansville, IN 47710
(812) 425-4642
●Healthy Life Breads

Life Services Supplements, Inc.
3535 Hwy 66 Bldg. #2
Neptune, NJ 07753
800-542-3230
732-922-5329 fax
www.lifeservices.com
●Asst. house brand foods,
drinks, mixes, nutritionals

Lindora, Inc.
3505 Cadillac Ave. Suite N2
Costa Mesa, CA 92626
800-LINDORA
714-668-9341 fax
www.leanforlife.com
●house brand soup mixes,
drink mixes

Low Carb Connoisseur
Enrich Enterprises, Inc.
1208 N. Main St.
Anderson, NC 29621
864-224-0245
864-419-9631
www.low-carb.com
●Asst. foods, nutritionals,
candies

Low Carb Dieter's Page
PO Box 92
Winter Park, FL 32790
407-644-5981 fax
www.lowcarbdieters.com
●Asst. foods, books, unique
products

Low Carb Living Market
1465 Encinitas Blvd. Suite H
Encinitas, CA 92024
760-634-5316
760-753-6315 fax
www.lowcarbliving.com
●Asst. foods

Low Carb Nexus
116 E. main St. Suite E
Jamestown, NC 27272
336-812-8845
336-812-8847 fax
www.lowcarbnexus.com
•Asst. foods, nutritionals
and house brand foods

McNeil Specialty Products Inc.
New Brunswick, NJ
800-SPLENDA
www.splenda.com
•Splenda granular and
packets

Morico Health Products
2102 Kotter Ave.
Evansville, IN 47715
800-524-4473
812-485-0006 fax
www.morico.com/locarb.html
•House brand ice cream,
baking, drink, bread mixes

Netrition
20 Petra Lane
Albany, NY 12205
888-817-2411
518-456-9673 fax
www.netrition.com
•Asst. foods, nutritionals

Nuts4U
PO Box 1864
Sugar Land. TX 77487
800-nuts4u2
www.nuts4u.com
•Asst. nuts and nut flours

Steels Gourmet Foods, Inc.
Continental Business Center
Suite D-175
Bridgeport, PA 19405
1-800-6-STEELS
610-277-1228
www.steelsgourmet.com
•Nature Sweet maltitol
•Splenda and maltitol
sweetened jams, syrups,
sauces and condiments

Stevita Stevia Co., Inc.
7650 US Hwy. 287 #100
Arlington, TX 76001
888-STEVITA
www.stevitastevia.htm
•Stevita brand stevia

Sugar Free Paridise
18747 W. Dixie Hwy.
N. Miami Beach, FL 33180
800-991-7888
305-682-8222 fax
www.sugarfreeparadise.com
•Asst. foods and house
brands

SynergyDiet
234 N. Allen Ave.
Pasadena, CA 91106
877-877-1558
626-229-0624 fax
www.synergydiet.com
www.zerocarb.com
•Asst. foods, candies

MORE . . .

www.lowcarbchocolates.com

www.lowcarboliscious.com

www.naturesflavors.com

www.optimumnutr.com

www.lowcarboutfitters.com

www.lowcarbcenter.com

www.traderjoes.com

www.lowcarbgrocery.com

www.steelsgourmet.com

www.fiberrich.bigstep.com

www.microwaveporkrinds.com

www.robbinsnest.org

www.carbsolutions.com

www.dixiediner.com

www.locarbdiner.com

www.davincigourmet.com

www.carbhealthmagazine.com

www.puredeliteproducts.com

www.specialcheese.com

www.toddsorganicbread.com

www.locarbcorner.com

www.carbsense.com

www.asherschocolates.com

www.eatalmonds.com

www.latortillafactory.com

www.optimumnutr.com

www.splenda.com

www.nuttyguys.com

Helpful measurements:

3 teaspoons = 1 tablespoon

2 tablespoons = 1 ounce

12 teaspoons = 4 tablespoons = 1/4 cup

24 teaspoons = 8 tablespoons = 1/2 cup

48 teaspoons = 16 tablespoons = 1 cup

5-1/3 tablespoons = 1/3 cup

1 cup = 1/2 pint = 8 ounces

2 cups = 1 pint = 16 ounces

4 cups = 2 pints = 1 quart = 32 ounces

8 cups = 2 quarts = 1/2 gallon = 64 ounces

16 cups = 4 quarts = 1 gallon = 128 ounces

---

8 drops = 1/8 teaspoon
16 drops = 1/4 teaspoon
32 drops = 1/2 teaspoon
64 drops = 1 teaspoon
192 drops = 1 tablespoon
384 drops = 1/8 cup (2 tablespoons)

---

1 quart casserole = 9" pie plate = 8" round pan = 7½ x 3½ x 2½ " loaf pan = 6" soufflé dish

1½ quart casserole = 10" pie plate = 9" round pan = 8½ x 3½ x 2½" loaf pan = 7" soufflé dish

2 quart casserole = 8 x 8 x 2" pan = 11 x 7 x 1½" pan = 9 x 5 x 3"loaf pan = 8" soufflé dish

2½ quart casserole = 9 x 9 x 2" pan = 11¾ x 7½ x 1¼" pan
3 quart casserole = 8 x 8 x 3½" pan = 13½ x 8½ x 2" glass dish

Sugar Substitute Equivalencies

Sugar	Splenda®, Sweet 'n Low ®, Equal ® Packets	Splenda ®, Sugar Twin®, Equal ® Granular/ Brown	Splenda® Tablets	Sweet 'n Low ® Liquid *check other brands	Nature Sweet® Crystals** (Steels Gourmet®)	Stevia Packets	Stevita ® Liquid *check other brands	Stevia Powder - Liquid U-Mix See page 27
1 teaspoon	1/2	1 tsp.	1	10 drops	1 tsp.	1/2	1/6 tsp.	4 drops
1 tablespoon	1-1/2	1 TBSP.	3	30 drops	1 TBSP.	1-1/2	1/2 tsp.	12 drops
1/4 cup	6	1/4 cup	12	1-1/2 tsp.	1/4 cup	6	2 tsp.	3/4 tsp.
1/3 cup	8	1/3 cup	16	2 tsp.	1/3 cup	8	2-2/3 tsp.	1 tsp.
1/2 cup	12	1/2 cup	24	1 TBSP.	1/2 cup	12	4 tsp.	1-1/2 tsp.
2/3 cup	16	2/3 cup	32	4 tsp.	2/3 cup	16	5-1/3 tsp.	2 tsp.
3/4 cup	18	3/4 cup	36	4-1/2 tsp.	3/4 cup	18	6 tsp.	2-1/4 tsp.
1 cup	24	1 cup	48	2 TBSP.	1 cup	24	8 tsp.	1 TBSP.

** If using Nature Sweet® Crystals, you can omit not/Sugar® in recipe

Notes

Frequently Asked Questions

- Blanching Almonds – how do I do it?
- Do sugar substitutes have carbs?
- Fearn® soya powder - is it the same as soy flour?
- not/Starch® - how do I use it?
- Nut Flour - how do I make it?
- Oat Flour - how do I make it?
- Splenda®- what is it?
- Steaming Cauliflower – how do I do it?
- Why are brand names listed in some recipes?
- Can I use Stevia as a sugar substitute?
- Xanthan gum - what is it?
- not/Sugar® - what is it?
- Can soy flour be substituted for a soy baking mix?
- What is Maltitol?
- What are Net Carbs?

Notes

Blanching Almonds – how do I do it?

Drop almonds into a pan of boiling water and cook for 30-45 seconds. Remove and drain. Cool with cold water. To remove almond skins, squeeze each between fingers. Dry by placing on cookie sheet and baking at 375° for 2-3 minutes. Cool before grinding. (Almonds do not have to be blanched before grinding. This is a personal preference.)

Do sugar substitutes have carbs?

Yes. However, the carbs come from the fillers being used in the particular substitute form. Granular form has more carbs than packets. Packets have more carbs than tablets. And liquid form has the fewest carbs, and sometimes zero. Check the labels. (Sugar substitutes always taste better when two different types are used together instead of a single source.) Maltitol has carbs but they are from sugar alcohols which have a minimal impact on blood sugar and are therefore subtracted when calculation Net Carbs.

Fearn® soya powder - is it the same as soy flour?

No. Soy flour is made by grinding whole dry soybeans into flour in the same way wheat kernels are ground into flour. It often contains considerable hull material, is more coarse, and may even be raw. Soy flour is often dry-toasted after grinding to improve the flavor and digestibility. Soya powder is made by cooking the soybeans before grinding. It is finer than soy flour and usually has a better flavor.

not/Starch® - how do I use it?

1 teaspoon of not/Starch® is equal to 1 teaspoon of cornstarch. However, if more than 1 teaspoon of cornstarch is to be substituted, start with ONLY 1 teaspoon of not/Starch® and sprinkle in more as needed. It does not need heat to thicken, just time. If a recipe has thickened too much, add additional liquid to thin.

Nut Flour - how do I make it?

Place nuts in blender, food processor or coffee grinder. (Use only small amounts at a time.) Grind until flour or meal consistency. You may want to sift out the larger pieces to either discard or re-grind.

Oat Flour - how do I make it?

Place regular oatmeal (not instant) in blender, food processor or coffee grinder. (Use only small amounts at a time.) Grind until flour or meal consistency. You may want to sift out the larger pieces to either discard or re-grind.

Splenda®- what is it?

It comes in granular, packet and tablet forms. Each form has different carb counts. Be sure to check the package or see page 21. (Sugar substitutes always taste better when two different types are used together instead of a single source.) Be sure to use not/Sugar® with Splenda® to get a closer texture to real sugar.

Steaming Cauliflower – how do I do it?

Place head or flowerettes in 1-1/2 quart microwaveable dish. Add 1/2 cup water and cover. Microwave for 5 minutes on high. Turn or stir pieces. Recover and microwave additional 5 minutes. Check for tenderness and adjust time as necessary for your microwave.

Why are brand names listed in some recipes?

Not all brands of the same food item have the same carb counts, fiber counts or taste. If a particular brand has the best combination of these three attributes, I will name it.

Can I use Stevia as a sugar substitute?

Yes. White stevia powder is the easiest to work with. However, the pure powder is 200 to 300 times the sweetness of sugar. For a more usable form, mix 2 tsp. White stevia powder with 2 TBSP. warmed water. Stir until dissolved and store in the refrigerator. See chart on page 21 for usage. (Sugar substitutes always taste better when two different types are used together instead of a single source.) Be sure to use not/Sugar® with stevia to get a closer texture to real sugar.

Xanthan gum - what is it?

Xanthan gum is used to help non-gluten flours rise. It can also be used to give a smooth, creamy texture to sauces. It has a unique ability to hold particles of food together, making it a good stabilizer.

not/Sugar® - what is it?

not/Sugar® is a vegetable fiber substance used to replace the bulk and mouthfeel of sugar. Sugar substitutes have no volume and contribute nothing to the texture. It does not change the taste in any way. Recipes in this book can be made without this ingredient without effecting the taste. (This product can be purchased on the Internet – manufacturer's web site is www.ExpertFoods.com – and now at many health food stores.) You do not need to use this with maltitol.

Can soy flour be substituted for a soy baking mix?

No. Soy flour is simply soy flour. A Soy Baking Mix is a mix of soy flour and leavening agents to help it rise. (Think of the difference between wheat flour and Bisquick® Baking Mix. However, Bisquick® also has fat mixed in it.) We suggest using Carbsense™ Zero Carb Baking Mix.

What is Maltitol?

Maltitol (Nature Sweet® brand) is a sugar substitute made from corn. It is in the family of sugar alcohols. Many low carb products use maltitol because it has a minimal impact on blood sugar. It is available in crystal (like sugar, brown sugar and powdered sugar) and liquid (like honey) forms. Maltitol is a one-for-one replacement for sugar. You do not need to add not/Sugar® to the recipe for proper texture.

What are Net Carbs?

Net Carbs are figured by taking the total carbohydrate grams and subtracting the fiber grams and the sugar alcohol grams. The final number is the Net Grams. This is the number used in counting your daily carb intake. Fiber and sugar alcohols are subtracted because they have a minimal impact on blood sugar.

NOTE: The Carbohydrates in this book are calculated using Splenda® as the sweetener. If you choose to use another sweetener, your actual carb count may be higher or lower.

APPETIZERS
and
SNACKS

Beef and Pecan Spread
Dill Dip
Cinnamon Almonds
Salmon Spread
Crab Dip
Hot Artichoke Dip
Crab Rangoon
Sausage Balls
Fried Cheese Crisps
Savory Nut Mix
Mom's Deviled Eggs
Mom's Spinach Dip
Onion Puffs
Sesame Cheddar Spread
Uncle David's Cheese Ball
Spicy Pecans

Fast & Easy Tips

- Macadamia nuts are the easiest snacks.

- Pumpkorn® is prepackaged and easy to pack. Check your local health food store.

- Always keep pork rinds on hand for the munchies – in several different flavors.

- Cheese balls are easy and low in carbs. Serve with pork rinds, Wasa Crisps® or celery sticks.

- Nuts are fast and easy for snacks, but watch the carb counts.

Beef and Pecan Spread
Serves 10

1/2	cup	pecans, unsalted -- chopped
1	teaspoon	unsalted butter
8	ounces	chipped beef
2	tablespoons	half & half
1/4	cup	green pepper -- chopped
1/2	teaspoon	garlic salt
1/2	cup	sour cream
8	ounces	cream cheese
2	teaspoons	dried minced onion flakes

Sauté the pecans in butter until warm. Set aside. Cut the chipped beef into small pieces. Blend the remaining ingredients in a food processor. Place mixture in a glass pie pan and sprinkle with pecans.

Bake at 350° for 20 minutes or until bubbly.

Per 1/10th recipe:	3 g carbs	1 g fiber	9 g protein
Food Exchanges:	3 fat + 1 lean meat		

Dill Dip
Serves 10

1	cup	Hellman's® mayonnaise
1	cup	sour cream
2	teaspoons	dried minced onion flakes
2	teaspoons	seasoned salt
2	teaspoons	dried dill weed

Combine all ingredients. Mix well. Chill before serving.

Per 1/10th serving:	1 g carbs	0 g fiber	1 g protein
Food Exchanges:	2-1/2 fat		

Cinnamon Almonds
Serves 8

1		egg white
1	teaspoon	ground cinnamon
	pinch	salt
1	cup	almonds
1/2	cup	granular sugar substitute — see page 21

Mix egg white, cinnamon and salt in medium bowl. Add almonds and mix until coated evenly. Add sugar substitute and mix well.

Spread on ungreased cookie sheet and bake at 325° for 15 minutes, shaking occasionally. Cool before serving.

Per 1/8th recipe:	4 g carbs	2 g fiber	4 g protein

Food Exchanges: 1/2 Starch + 1-1/2 Fat + 1/2 Lean Meat

Salmon Spread
Serves 10

31	ounces	canned salmon -- drained
8	ounces	cream cheese -- softened
3	teaspoons	onion -- grated
1	tablespoon	ReaLemon® lemon juice
1/4	teaspoon	liquid smoke flavoring
1/4	teaspoon	salt
2	teaspoons	Worcestershire sauce
	pinch	horseradish

Mix all ingredients well. Chill before serving.

Per 1/10th recipe:	1 g carbs	0 g fiber	19 g protein

Food Exchanges: 1-1/2 fat + 2 Lean Meat

Crab Dip

Serves 16

1	pound	crab meat
16	ounces	cream cheese -- softened
1	cup	sour cream
4	tablespoons	Hellman's® mayonnaise
1	tablespoon	ReaLemon® lemon juice
1	tablespoon	Worcestershire sauce
1/2	teaspoon	hot sauce
1/2	teaspoon	garlic salt
1	cup	cheddar cheese -- shredded

Combine all the ingredients except 1/2 cup cheddar cheese. Place in baking dish. Sprinkle remaining cheddar cheese on top.

Bake at 325° for 30 minutes. Garnish with parsley flakes.

Per 1/16th recipe:	2 g carbs	0 g fiber	10 g protein

Food Exchanges:	3 Fat + 1-1/2 Lean Meat

Hot Artichoke Dip

Serves 10

8-1/2	ounces (net)	canned artichoke hearts -- drained
1	cup	Hellman's® mayonnaise
1	cup	Parmesan cheese
1	clove	garlic -- crushed
1	tablespoon	ReaLemon® lemon juice
1/4	cup	almond slivers

Combine all ingredients except almonds. Sprinkle almonds on top.

Bake at 350° for 20 minutes or until hot and bubbly.

Per 1/10th recipe:	4 g carbs	2 g fiber	5 g protein

Food Exchanges:	2 Fat + 1/2 Lean Meat + 1/2 Vegetable

Crab Rangoon
Serves 4

8	ounces	cream cheese -- softened
6	ounces	crab meat
1	tablespoon	dried minced onion flakes
2	teaspoons	dried chives

Mix all ingredients together. Chill before serving.

Per 1/4th recipe: 3 g carbs   0 g fiber   13 g protein

Food Exchanges: 3-1/2 Fat + 2 Lean Meat

Sausage Balls
Serves 16

1	cup	Carbsense® Zero Carb Baking Mix
1	pound	pork sausage
16	ounces	cheddar cheese -- shredded
1/2	cup	Parmesan cheese
1/2	teaspoon	dried rosemary
1/2	teaspoon	dried parsley

Mix all ingredients well. (Add more soy mix for desired consistency, if necessary.) Shape into 1-inch balls. Place in ungreased shallow baking dish.

Bake at 350° for 20-25 minutes or until browned. Remove from pan immediately. Makes about 8 dozen.

Per 1/16th recipe: 2 g carbs   1 g fiber   17 g protein

Food Exchanges: 3-1/2 fat + 1-1/2 Lean Meat

Fried Cheese Crisps
Serves 4

| 4 | ounces | cheddar cheese -- shredded |
| | | olive oil spray |

Spray a non-stick pan with the oil. Spread grated cheese over bottom of pan. Fry until brown; flip over and continue frying for about 1 minute. Drain on paper towel.

Per 1/4th recipe: 1/2 g carbs   0 g fiber   7 g protein

Food Exchanges: 1 Fat + 1 Lean Meat

Optional: Crumble bacon bits into cheese before frying.

Savory Nut Mix
Serves 12

1	cup	walnuts
1	cup	almonds
1	cup	pecans
1/2	cup	butter
3	tablespoons	Worcestershire sauce
1	teaspoon	garlic salt

Boil nuts in water for 5 minutes. Drain and set aside.

Melt butter with Worcestershire sauce and garlic salt in medium sauce pan. Add nuts, mixing well to coat.

Spread nut mixture on ungreased cookie sheet. Bake at 350° until nuts are crisp.

Per 1/12th recipe: 6 g carbs   2 g fiber   4 g protein

Food Exchanges: 4-1/2 fat + 1/2 Lean Meat + 1/2 Starch

Mom's Deviled Eggs
Serves 24

12		eggs -- boiled and cooled
1/3	cup	Hellman's® mayonnaise
1	teaspoon	prepared mustard
		salt -- to taste
		pepper -- to taste
		ground paprika -- for garnish

Cut hard boiled eggs in half. Scoop out the yolks. Mix mayonnaise, mustard, salt and pepper with the yolks. Divide the yolk mixture among the egg halves. Sprinkle with paprika before serving.

Per 1/2 egg: 1/2 g carbs   0g fiber   3 g protein

Food Exchanges: 1/2 Fat + 1/2 Lean Meat

Mom's Spinach Dip
Serves 8

10	ounces	frozen chopped spinach -- thawed & drained
1/4	cup	onion -- chopped
5	ounces	water chestnuts -- drained & chopped
1	cup	Hellman's® mayonnaise
1	cup	sour cream
1	envelope	Knorrs® Vegetable Soup Mix

Mix all ingredients well. Refrigerate before serving.

Per 1/8th recipe: 8 g carbs   2 g fiber   3 g protein

Food Exchanges: 3 fat + 1/2 Starch + 1/2 Vegetable

Onion Puffs
Serves 24

1/2	cup	water
1/4	cup	unsalted butter
1	envelope	Kroger® Onion Soup Mix
2	teaspoons	caraway seeds
1	teaspoon	dry mustard
1/3	cup	Carbsense® Zero Carb Baking Mix
1	cup	Swiss cheese -- shredded
2		eggs

Bring water, butter, soup mix, caraway seeds and mustard to a boil in medium sauce pan. Reduce heat, add soy mix and stir vigorously until soft dough forms. Remove from heat and beat in cheese and eggs until smooth and cheese is almost melted.

Drop by spoonfuls (24) on greased cookie sheet about 2 inches apart.

Bake at 375° for 10-12 minutes or until puffed.

Per puff: 1 g carbs   0 g fiber   3 g protein

Food Exchanges: 1/2 Fat + 1/2 Lean Meat

Sesame Cheddar Spread
Serves 10

8	ounces	cream cheese -- softened
1	cup	cheddar cheese -- shredded
1	tablespoon	soy sauce
2	tablespoons	sesame seeds -- toasted

Blend cheeses together. Stir in soy sauce and mix until smooth. Stir in the sesame seeds.

(Add 1-2 tablespoons of sour cream if softer spread is desired.)

Per 1/10th recipe:	1 g carbs	0 g fiber	5 g protein

Food Exchanges:	2 fat + 1/2 Lean Meat

Optional: For a dip, substitute 1-1/2 cups of sour cream for the cream cheese.

For a cheese ball, combine all the ingredients except the sesame seeds. Form a ball and roll in the sesame seeds.)

Uncle David's Cheese Ball
Serves 12

5	ounces	Kraft® Old English Cheese Spread
4	ounces	blue cheese wedge, crumbled
16	ounces	cream cheese -- softened
1/2	cup	onion -- chopped fine
1/4	cup	pecans -- chopped

Mix ingredients (except pecans) well and shape into a ball. Roll in crushed pecans. Chill before serving.

Per 1/12th recipe:	3 g carbs	0 g fiber	7 g protein

Food Exchanges:	3-1/2 fat + 1 Lean Meat

Spicy Pecans
Serves 10

1	tablespoon	oil
2	tablespoons	unsalted butter
1	tablespoon	Worcestershire sauce
1/2	teaspoon	Tabasco sauce
3/4	teaspoon	ground cumin
1/2	teaspoon	ground paprika
1/2	teaspoon	garlic powder
2	cups	pecan halves
2	teaspoons	coarse salt

Heat oil and butter in medium sauce pan over low heat until melted. Add the spices (except salt) and mix well. Add nuts and toss to coat.

Spread on ungreased cookie sheet and bake at 325° for 15 minutes, shaking occasionally.

Toss the nuts with the salt. Let cool to room temperature, then store in airtight container. Makes about 2 cups.

Per 1/10th recipe:	4 g carbs	2 g fiber	2 g protein

Food Exchanges: 3-1/2 Fat + 1/2 Starch

Favorite Recipes

BREADS

Cheese Biscuits
Cheese Crackers
Bread I
Bread II
Sausage Muffins
Zucchini Bread
Cheese Crackers II

Fast & Easy Tips

- Buying Healthy Life® 100% Whole Wheat Bread is by far the easiest and best solution.

- Bake the Bread I or Bread II and freeze 2 pieces in a package.

- Try the low carb whole wheat tortillas from La Tortilla Factory® for a great bread substitute. See page 17 for details.

Cheese Biscuits

Serves 18

3		eggs -- slightly beaten
1-1/2	cups	Carbsense® Zero Carb Baking Mix
1/8	cup	oil
1/2	cup	half & half
1/4	cup	water
1-1/2	teaspoons	butter extract
3	ounces	cheddar cheese -- shredded
2	tablespoons	baking powder
1	teaspoon	xanthan gum

Mix all ingredients except water well. Add water 1 tablespoon at a time, don't let dough get too thin. Drop by tablespoonfuls (18) onto greased cookie sheet.

Bake at 350° for 10-12 minutes or until slightly golden.

Per biscuit: 2 g carbs   1 g fiber   8 g protein

Food Exchanges: 1/2 fat + 1 Lean Meat

Cheese Crackers I
Serves 24

3	ounces	cream cheese -- softened
3	ounces	sharp cheddar cheese -- grated
1		egg
1/2	cup	Fearn® Soya Powder
1/2	teaspoon	salt
		ground paprika

Beat cream cheese, cheddar cheese, egg, soya powder and salt together in a small mixing bowl. Chill dough. Shape mixture into 24 walnut sized balls. Place on well greased cookie sheet. Gently flatten with hand. Sprinkle with paprika.

Bake at 375° for 15-20 minutes or until slightly browned.

Per cracker: 1 g carbs   0 g fiber   2 g protein

Food Exchanges: 1/2 Fat + 1/2 Lean Meat

Bread I
(for use in French Toast or Bread Pudding — see page 135)
Serves 12 (1 loaf)

6		eggs
1/4	teaspoon	cream of tartar
1	teaspoon	granular sugar substitute — see page 21
1/4	cup	Carbsense® Zero Carb Baking Mix
1/4	cup	ground almonds — see page 26

Separate eggs and place yolks and whites in two large bowls. Beat the whites, cream of tartar and sugar substitute until stiff peaks form. Beat yolks, then add soy mix and ground almonds and blend well. Add enough whites to yolk mixture to make batter the consistency of thick cake batter. Fold yolk mixture into remaining whites. Blend well but do not beat down whites. Spoon batter into well greased 8" loaf pan.

Bake at 350° for 30-40 minutes, turning after 15 minutes. Leave bread in pan for 5 minutes to set up. Remove from pan and cool on cooling rack, top side up.

Slice into 12 pieces. Can be frozen if 1-2 slices wrapped with plastic wrap.

| Per slice: | 1 g carbs | 0 g fiber | 5 g protein |

| Food Exchanges: | 1/2 Fat + 1/2 Lean Meat |

Bread II
Serves 36 (3 loaves)

1-1/2	cups	water
1-1/2	cups	half & half
2	tablespoons	unsalted butter -- softened
1	tablespoon	granular sugar substitute — see page 21
1/2	teaspoon	salt
2		eggs -- beaten
3-1/3	cups	Bob's Red Mill® Vital Wheat Gluten Flour
2/3	cup	oat flour — see page 26
1	package	active dry yeast -- fast rising
1	teaspoon	sugar

If using a bread machine, set on dough cycle and add ingredients in the order listed above. Let machine complete only the mixing cycle. Remove from machine and divide into three equal parts. Shape into loaves and place in three 8" loaf pans. Let rise until double.

Bake at 350° for 35-45 minutes or until done in the middle. (Hint: Thump on the bottom of loaf, it should sound hollow when done.) Leave bread in pan for 5 minutes to set up. Remove from pan and cool on cooling rack, top side up.

Slice into each loaf into 12 pieces. Discard the ends, they will be too tough.

Per slice:	4 g carbs	0 g fiber	9 g protein

Food Exchanges: 1/2 fat + 1-1/2 Lean Meat

Optional: If mixing by hand, add yeast to 105-115° water to dissolve. (Water too hot will kill the yeast.) Add half & half, butter and egg. Mix well. Add sugar substitute, salt, oat flour and vital wheat gluten. Dough will be like batter bread. Divide into three equal parts. Shape into loaves and place in three 8" loaf pans. Let rise until double. Bake.

Sausage Muffins
Serves 12

1	pound	sausage
6		eggs -- separated
1	cup	Carbsense® Zero Carb Baking Mix
1	teaspoon	baking powder
1	teaspoon	salt
1/2	cup	Hellman's® mayonnaise
1/2	cup	sour cream
4	ounces	cheddar cheese -- shredded
1	teaspoon	xanthan gum

Spray muffin tins with Pam or use paper liners. Cook sausage, drain and crumble. Separate eggs, set whites aside and beat yolks. Add soy mix, baking powder, salt, mayonnaise, sour cream, cheese and xanthan gum to yolks. Blend with spoon, mix will be stiff. Add sausage to mixture. Beat the egg whites until stiff. Gently fold whites into sausage mixture.

Spoon into 12 muffin tins and bake at 375° for 30 minutes.

Per muffin:	3 g carbs	1 g fiber	15 g protein

Food Exchanges: 4-1/2 Fat + 2 Lean Meat

Zucchini Bread
Serves 2

2	slices	Healthy Life® 100% Whole Wheat Bread
2		eggs
1/4	cup	half & half
1	teaspoon	baking soda
	dash	salt
1	teaspoon	ground cinnamon
1	teaspoon	vanilla extract
1/4	teaspoon	ground nutmeg
1/4	teaspoon	ground cloves
1	tablespoon	granular sugar substitute — see page 21
1	cup	zucchini -- peeled and grated

Process bread in blender until fine crumbs. Place in medium bowl and mix in remaining ingredients until smooth. Pour into 2 4x6" greased loaf pans.

Bake at 350° for 30 minutes.

Per 1/2 recipe: 10 g carbs   4 g fiber   7 g protein

Food Exchanges: 1 Fat + 1 Lean Meat + 1 Starch

Cheese Crackers II
Serves 48

1/2	cup	unsalted butter — softened
8	ounces	sharp Cheddar Cheese — shredded
1/4	teaspoon	salt
1/8	teaspoon	ground cayenne pepper
1-1/8	cup	Fearn® Soya Powder
1	teaspoon	xanthan gum
2	cups	pecan halves

In medium mixing bowl, combine butter, shredded cheese, salt and cayenne pepper. Mix well. Stir in soya powder and xanthan gum. Shape dough into 3 rolls about 1-1/2 inches in diameter. Wrap roll in plastic wrap and chill until firm. Remove rolls from refrigerator, remove plastic wrap and cut into 1/4 inch slices (about 16 per roll). Place each slice on parchment paper lined cookie sheet. Press a pecan half into each slice.

Bake at 375° for 10-12 minutes. Cool before storing in airtight container.

Per cracker: 2 g carbs   1 g fiber   2 g protein

Food Exchanges: 1-1/2 Fat + 1/2 Lean Meat

Favorite Recipes

SOUPS
and
SAUCES

Broccoli Cheese Soup
Chili
Chunky Chicken Soup
Cream of Broccoli Soup
Cream of Chicken Soup
Egg Drop Soup
French-Style Onion Soup

Cheese Sauce
Mustard Sauce
Chocolate Sauce I
Chocolate Sauce II
Parsley Mushroom Gravy

Fast & Easy Tips

- For a quick soup, try chicken bouillon with canned chicken.

- Canned soup is fast but the carb counts are high. Try eating a very small portion as a side instead of as the meal itself.

- Five Brothers® Alfredo Sauce in a jar is not or fast and easy but wonderful. At only 2 grams carb per 1/4 cup, put it on everything.

- If the half & half or sour cream in your soup separates or curdles from overheating, strain the liquid into the blender. Blend for a minute and return to the soup.

- It's easy to convert any recipe calling for milk for every cup of milk, substitute 1/2 cup half half and 1/2 cup water.

Broccoli Cheese Soup
Serves 8

2	cups	broccoli florets --blanched & chopped
4	cups	Swanson's® Fat-Free Chicken Broth
4	ounces	cream cheese -- softened
1/2	teaspoon	Worcestershire sauce
1	cup	cheddar cheese -- shredded
1/4	cup	Parmesan cheese
		salt -- to taste
		pepper -- to taste
1/3	cup	half & half

Drop broccoli in boiling water for about 3 minutes, rinse with cold water and chop. Set aside. Heat chicken broth on low heat just until boil. Add cream cheese in small pieces and stir until blended. Add broccoli, Worcestershire sauce, cheeses, salt and pepper. Stir until blended. Add half & half and heat for about 1 minute. Do not boil.

Per 1/8th recipe: 2 g carbs   1 g fiber   7 g protein

Food Exchanges: 2 Fat + 1 Lean Meat

Chili
Serves 4

1	pound	ground beef -- cooked and drained
1/4	teaspoon	celery salt
1/4	teaspoon	pepper
14	ounces	beef broth -- canned
4	ounces	tomato sauce -- canned
2	teaspoons	chili powder
1/4	cup	onion -- chopped
1	teaspoon	ground cumin
1-1/2	teaspoons	ground paprika
3/4	teaspoon	garlic powder
1/2	teaspoon	granular brown sugar substitute – see page 21

Cook and drain ground beef. Crumble. Sprinkle celery salt and pepper over cooked beef. stir well. Add beef broth and tomato sauce. Bring to boil, reduce heat to low. Add remaining ingredients. Stir well. Simmer for 20 minutes.

Per 1/4th recipe:	6 g carbs	1 g fiber	24 g protein

Food Exchanges: 4-1/2 Fat + 3 Lean Meat + 1/2 Vegetable

Optional: Serve with shredded cheese on top.

Chunky Chicken Soup
Serves 4

4		chicken breast halves without skin
4	cups	Swanson's® Fat-Free Chicken Broth
1/2	cup	celery -- chopped
1/2	cup	onion -- chopped
		salt -- to taste
		pepper -- to taste

Chop chicken breast into small, bite size pieces.

Bring chicken broth to boil. Reduce heat and add chicken, celery and onion. Salt and pepper to taste. Simmer for at least 30 minutes, or until vegetables are tender.

Per 1/4th recipe: 3 g carbs   1 g fiber   23 g protein

Food Exchanges: 4 Lean Meat + 1/2 Vegetable

Cream of Broccoli Soup
Serves 6

3	cups	broccoli florets
3/4	cup	onion -- chopped
3/4	cup	celery -- chopped
1	cup	unsalted butter
1/4	cup	Fearn® Soya Powder
3/4	cup	half & half
3	cups	Swanson's® Fat-Free Chicken Broth
1/2	cup	whipping cream
1	teaspoon	not/Starch®
	dash	ground nutmeg
		salt -- to taste
		pepper -- to taste

Drop broccoli in boiling water for about 3 minutes, rinse with cold water and chop. Set aside. Sauté onion and celery in butter. Stir in soya powder until well blended.

Combine the half & half, chicken broth and broccoli. Working with a portion at a time, pulverize this mixture in the blender. Return mixture to a saucepan with onion and celery. Sprinkle in not/Starch® until desired thickness – you may not use it all. Simmer until thickened. Add whipping cream, nutmeg, salt and pepper.

Per 1/6th recipe: 8 g carbs 3 g fiber 5 g protein

Food Exchanges: 8-1/2 Fat + 1 Vegetable

Cream of Chicken Soup
Serves 4

1/4	cup	celery -- chopped
2	tablespoons	unsalted butter
4	cups	Swanson's® Fat-Free Chicken Broth
12	ounces	canned chicken -- drained
1/2	teaspoon	dried parsley
		pepper -- to taste
		salt -- to taste
1-1/2	cups	half & half
1	teaspoon	not/Starch®

Sauté celery in butter. Add chicken broth and bring to a boil. Reduce heat and add chicken, parsley, salt and pepper. Simmer for 10 minutes. Remove from heat and stir in half & half. Sprinkle in not/Starch® until desired thickness – you may not use it all. Reheat on low but do not boil.

Per 1/4th recipe: 5 g carbs   1 g fiber   24 g protein

Food Exchanges: 3-1/2 Fat + 2-1/2 Lean Meat + 1/2 Non-Fat Milk

Egg Drop Soup
Serves 8

1	tablespoon	cornstarch
1/4	cup	water
1/4	teaspoon	granular sugar substitute — see page 21
1/4	teaspoon	Accent® seasoning mix
3/4	teaspoon	salt
5	cups	Swanson's® Fat-Free Chicken Broth
2		eggs
2		scallions -- chopped
2	teaspoons	sesame oil

Mix cornstarch with water. In large pan, mix sugar substitute, Accent® and salt with chicken broth. Bring to rapid boil. Stir until no longer cloudy.

Beat eggs in a small bowl until foamy. Slowly swirl in beaten eggs. Do not stir. Turn off heat. Drop in scallions and sesame oil. Mix gently. Serve hot.

Per 1/8th recipe: 2 g carbs   0 g fiber   2 g protein

Food Exchanges: 1/2 Fat

French-Style Onion Soup
Serves 6

3	cups	onions
1	tablespoon	oil
1	tablespoon	Fearn® Soya Powder
1		garlic clove -- pressed
5	cups	Swanson's® Fat-Free Chicken Broth
1	tablespoon	soy sauce
1/2	cup	Swiss cheese -- shredded

Cut onions in half lengthwise, then slice into thin half-circles. Cook onions slowly in oil over low heat in covered skillet. Sprinkle soya powder over onions after they have started to turn golden. Add garlic. Continue cooking for 2-3 minutes or until thoroughly coated. Add chicken broth and soy sauce to mixture. Cover and cook for 15 minutes over low heat.

Pour into 6 oven-proof bowls and sprinkle each with cheese. Bake at 400°, or under broiler, just until cheese has melted.

Per 1/6th recipe: 8 g carbs   2 g fiber   5 g protein

Food Exchanges: 1 Fat + 1/2 Lean Meat + 1-1/2 Vegetable

Cheese Sauce
Serves 4

1/4	cup	unsalted butter
1/4	cup	Fearn® Soya Powder
1	cup	half & half
1	cup	water
1	teaspoon	Worcestershire sauce
1	teaspoon	salt
1/8	teaspoon	pepper
2-1/2	cups	cheddar cheese -- shredded
1	teaspoon	not/Starch®

Mix first 8 ingredients over low heat until blended. Sprinkle in not/
Starch® until desired thickness – you may not use it all.

Per 1/4th recipe:	6 g carbs	1 g fiber	22 g protein

Food Exchanges: 7 fat + 1-1/2 Lean Meat

Mustard Sauce
Serves 4

1/4	cup	water
6		scallions -- chopped
1	cup	Swanson's® Fat-Free Chicken Broth
1/3	cup	sour cream
1	teaspoon	not/Starch®
2	teaspoons	Dijon mustard

Boil water and scallions in small uncovered sauce pan until liquid is reduced to 2 tablespoons (about 2 minutes). Add chicken broth and boil
until liquid is reduced to 1 cup (about 2 minutes). Reduce heat to low
and add sour cream. Sprinkle in not/Starch® until desired thickness –
you may not use it all. Whisk for 1 minute. Stir in mustard.

Per 1/4th recipe:	3 g carbs	1 g fiber	2 g protein

Food Exchanges: 1 Fat + 1/2 Vegetable

Chocolate Sauce I
Serves 4

1	cup	ricotta cheese
1/4	cup	unsweetened cocoa powder
1/3	cup	granular sugar substitute — see page 21
1	teaspoon	vanilla extract
1	teaspoon	not/Sugar®
1	tablespoon	half & half

Blend all ingredients well, using half & half to obtain desired consistency.

Per 1/4th recipe: 6 g carbs   2 g fiber   5 g protein

Food Exchanges: 1/2 Fat + 1/2 Lean Meat

Chocolate Sauce II
Serves 8

3/4	cup	whipping cream
3/4	cup	unsweetened cocoa
2	tablespoons	unsalted butter
2	teaspoons	vanilla extract
	dash	salt
3/4	cup	granular sugar substitute — see page 21
1	teaspoon	not/Sugar®

Gradually stir half & half into the cocoa in a small sauce pan. Add butter and cook over medium heat to just simmering, stirring frequently. Stir in vanilla, sugar substitute, salt and not/Sugar®. Cool.

Per 1/8th recipe: 6 g carbs   3 g fiber   2 g protein

Food Exchanges: 2-1/2 Fat + 1/2 Starch

Parsley Mushroom Gravy

Serves 8

2	tablespoons	unsalted butter
4	tablespoons	Fear® Soya Powder
2	cups	Swanson's® Fat-Free Chicken Broth
1	teaspoon	not/Starch®
4	ounces	canned mushrooms -- drained
1	tablespoon	dried parsley
		salt -- to taste
		pepper -- to taste

Melt butter in small pan. Add soya powder and cook over medium heat, stirring constantly until golden. Add chicken broth slowly. Sprinkle in not/Starch® until desired thickness – you may not use it all. Bring to boil. Continue cooking until thickened, stirring constantly. Stir in remaining ingredients.

Per serving: 2 g carbs   1 g fiber   2 g protein

Food Exchanges: 1/2 Fat

BREAKFAST DISHES

Broccoli Cheese Eggs
Eggs & Bacon Dish
Maple Butter
Maple Syrup
Pancakes - Cinnamon
Pancakes - Chocolate
Sausage Casserole
Spinach Casserole
Waffles
Waffles - Chocolate
Ham Asparagus Bake

Fast & Easy Tips

- Be creative – add anything you desire to scrambled eggs. Add leftover vegetables or leftover meats.

- Who said you had to eat eggs for breakfast? Have a steak or ham or chicken.

- Craving cereal? Try not/Cereal® from Expert Foods (see page 16).

- Protein drinks are very fast and easy for breakfast. Many brands ands flavors are available. Try Atkins®, ProForMix® or Designer Whey Protein® mixes. Be sure to check labels for carb counts on other brands.

- Any recipe calling for milk can be easily substituted. 1 cup milk = 1/2 cup half & half and 1/2 cup water.

Broccoli Cheese Eggs
Serves 2

4		eggs -- beaten
2	tablespoons	half & half
		salt -- to taste
		pepper -- to taste
1	tablespoon	unsalted butter
1/2	cup	cheddar cheese -- shredded
1/4	cup	broccoli -- chopped

Mix the eggs with the half & half, salt and pepper. In a frying pan, melt the butter and add the eggs. Add the cheese and broccoli. Scramble. Serve hot.

Per 1/2 recipe:	3 g carbs	0 g fiber	19 g protein

Food Exchanges: 3-1/2 Fat + 2-1/2 Lean Meat

Eggs & Bacon Dish
Serves 6

12		eggs
1	tablespoon	half & half
1/2	pound	bacon
8	ounces	sour cream
1	cup	cheddar cheese -- shredded

Beat the eggs with a little half & half. Fry the bacon, drain and crumble. Place a layer of eggs in the bottom of a casserole dish. Spread with the sour cream. Top with cheese and bacon layers.

Bake at 350° for 20 minutes.

Per 1/6th recipe:	3 g carbs	0 fiber	28 g protein

Food Exchanges: 6 Fat + 4 Lean Meat

Maple Butter
Serves 8

1/2	cup	unsalted butter -- softened
1/2	teaspoon	maple extract
1/3	cup	granular sugar substitute — see page 21

Mix all ingredients well.

Per 1/8th recipe: 1/2 g carbs   0 fiber   1/2 g protein

Food Exchanges: 2-1/2 Fat

Maple Syrup
Serves 6

1-1/2	cups	water -- boiling
1	cup	granular sugar substitute — see page 21
2	teaspoons	maple extract
1/2	teaspoon	vanilla extract
3	tablespoons	butter
1/8	teaspoon	salt
1	teaspoon	not/Starch®

Mix first 6 ingredients in blender until smooth. Sprinkle in not/Starch® until desired thickness – you may not use it all. Heat before using. Can be stored in refrigerator in air-tight container.

Per 1/6th recipe: 1/2 g carbs   0 g fiber   1/2 g protein

Food Exchanges: 1 Fat

Pancakes - Cinnamon
Serves 8

1	cup	Fearn® Soya Powder -- sifted
2		eggs
1	teaspoon	vanilla extract
1	tablespoon	ground cinnamon
	dash	salt
1/2	cup	whipping cream
1/2	cup	water
1	teaspoon	baking powder
2	packets	sugar substitute — see page 21
1	teaspoon	xanthan gum
1/2	teaspoon	baking soda

Combine all ingredients except soya powder in mixing bowl. Sift powder into mixture. Ladle pancakes onto preheated and oiled griddle. Cook until firm on one side. Carefully turn and cook until browned.

Per 1/8th recipe: 5 g carbs   2 g fiber   7 g protein

Food Exchanges: 1-1/2 Fat + 1/2 Lean Meat + 1/2 Starch

Pancakes - Chocolate

Replace cinnamon with 2 tablespoons of unsweetened cocoa. Increase sugar substitute to 4 packets.

Per 1/8th recipe: 6 g carbs   3 g fiber   7 g protein

Food Exchanges: 1-1/2 Fat + 1/2 Lean Meat + 1/2 Starch

Sausage Casserole
Serves 8

1/2	cup	unsalted butter -- melted
1	pound	sausage
6	slices	Healthy Life® 100% Whole Wheat Bread -- cubed
2	teaspoons	dried basil
1	teaspoon	dried dill weed
1/2	cup	cheddar cheese -- shredded
6		eggs -- beaten
1	cup	half & half
1	cup	water

Pour melted butter into a 9x13" baking dish. Brown the sausage and set aside after draining and crumbling. Layer half the cubed bread in buttered baking dish and sprinkle with half the basil, dill and cheese. Repeat layers. Sprinkle with cooked sausage meat over finished layers. Add the half & half and water to the beaten eggs. Pour mixture over the contents of baking dish.

Bake at 350° for 30 minutes or until set.

Per 1/8th recipe:	7 g carbs	2 g fiber	14 g protein

Food Exchanges:	7-1/2 fat + 1/2 Starch

Spinach Casserole

Serves 6

1	pound	sausage
10	ounces	mushrooms -- sliced
1/4	cup	onion -- chopped
1/2	cup	green pepper -- chopped
10	ounces	frozen chopped spinach -- thawed & drained
6		eggs
1	teaspoon	dry mustard
1/2	cup	whipping cream
1	cup	sharp cheddar cheese -- shredded
		salt -- to taste
		pepper -- to taste

Brown sausage and crumble. Save the drippings. Set aside. Sauté mushrooms, onions and green peppers in the sausage drippings until mushrooms are cooked. Drain grease.

Lightly oil casserole dish. Spread spinach over bottom. Place sausage over spinach. Sprinkle mushroom, onion and green pepper mixture on top. Beat the eggs, mustard, whipping cream, salt and pepper together. Pour mixture over layers. Sprinkle cheese on top.

Cover and bake at 350° for 40 minutes. Uncover and bake 10-15 minutes more or until set.

Per 1/6th recipe: 8 g carbs   2 g fiber   22 g protein

Food Exchanges: 8 Fat + 2-1/2 Lean Meat + 1 Vegetable

Waffles

Serves 8

2/3	cup	Fearn® Soya Powder -- sifted
2		eggs
1	teaspoon	vanilla extract
	dash	salt
1	teaspoon	baking powder
1/2	cup	whipping cream
1	tablespoon	oil
2	packets	sugar substitute — see page 21
1	teaspoon	xanthan gum
1/2	teaspoon	baking soda

Mix all ingredients well. Dough will be stiff. Add water to adjust consistency. Use waffle iron in accordance with directions.

Per 1/8th recipe: 4 g carbs   2 g fiber   5 g protein

Food Exchanges: 2 Fat + 1/2 Lean Meat

Waffles - Chocolate

Increase vanilla to 2 teaspoons. Add 2 tablespoons of unsweetened cocoa. Increase sugar substitute to 1/2 cup.

Per 1/8th recipe: 4 g carbs   2 g fiber   5 g protein

Food Exchanges: 2 Fat + 1/2 Lean Meat

Ham Asparagus Bake
Serves 8

2	tablespoons	unsalted butter
3	tablespoons	scallions — sliced
1/2	pound	fresh asparagus — cut into 1/2" pieces
6		eggs
1/3	cup	half & half
1	teaspoon	dried mustard
1/4	teaspoon	pepper
2	cups	cooked ham — chopped
1-1/2	cups	Cheddar cheese — shredded

Melt butter in heavy skillet. Add scallions and asparagus pieces to skillet. Cook over medium heat for 3 minutes. In separate bowl, combine eggs, half & half and seasonings. Pour asparagus mix in greased 9 x 13" baking dish. Layer ham in baking dish. Pour egg mixture over ham layer.

Bake at 350° for 20 minutes. Spread shredded cheese over baked dish. Bake for another 10-15 minutes.

Per 1/8th recipe:	4 g carbs	1 g fiber	16 g protein

Food Exchanges:	2-1/2 Fat + 2 Lean Meat + 1/2 Vegetable

Favorite Recipes

SALADS

Broccoli Salad
Cauliflower Broccoli Salad
Chicken and Nut Salad
Dilled Croutons
Chicken and Watercress Salad
Cucumber Slices
Green Bean Salad with Sunflower Seeds
Green Bean Salad with Walnut Dressing
"Potato" Salad
Tuna and Nut Salad
Spinach Salad with Mustard Dressing

Fast & Easy Tips

- Grocery stores carry ready-to-eat salads in a bag. Watch out for the croutons.

- Most salad dressings are low in carbs. Read the labels. Don't get the low fat versions – they are higher in carbs.

- Get real bacon bits (0 carbs).

- Watch out for carrots. They are high in carbs – 1/2 cup shredded is 5.6 grams carb.

- Forget those rules you grew up with. You know the ones – always serve this with this and that with that. Be creative!

Broccoli Salad
Serves 8

1/2	pound	bacon
4	cups	broccoli florets
1/2	cup	sharp cheddar cheese -- shredded
1/2	cup	red onion -- chopped
1/2	cup	Hellman's® mayonnaise
1/4	cup	granular sugar substitute — see page 21
1	teaspoon	vinegar

Cook, drain and crumble the bacon. Combine the broccoli, bacon, cheese and onion in large bowl. In separate bowl, mix the mayonnaise, sugar substitute and vinegar. Toss dressing with vegetables. Chill before serving.

Per 1/8th recipe: 4 g carbs   1 g fiber   12 g protein

Food Exchanges: 3-1/2 Fat + 1-1/2 Lean Meat + 1/2 Vegetable

Cauliflower Broccoli Salad
Serves 8

2	cups	broccoli florets
3	cups	cauliflower florets
1	pound	bacon -- fried and crumbled
1	cup	Hellman's® mayonnaise
1/3	cup	granular sugar substitute — see page 21
1/2	cup	buttermilk
3/4	cup	Parmesan cheese

In a large bowl, combine broccoli, cauliflower and bacon. Combine mayonnaise, sugar substitute, buttermilk and cheese. Toss dressing with vegetables. Chill before serving.

Per 1/8th recipe: 4 g carbs   1 g fiber   22 g protein

Food Exchanges: 6 Fat + 3 lean Meat + 1/2 Vegetable

Chicken and Nut Salad
Serves 4

12	ounces	canned chicken -- drained
1/2	cup	celery -- chopped
1/4	cup	walnuts -- chopped
1/2	cup	Hellman's® mayonnaise
1	tablespoon	dried dill weed
1	teaspoon	dried minced onion flakes
		salt -- to taste
		pepper -- to taste

Combine all ingredients in a small bowl. Mix well.

Per 1/4th recipe: 2 g carbs   1 g fiber   20 g protein

Food Exchanges: 2-1/2 Fat + 2-1/2 Lean Meat

Dilled Croutons
Serves 6

3	ounces	pork rinds
1/4	cup	oil
1/2	teaspoon	lemon pepper seasoning
1/2	teaspoon	garlic powder
1-1/2	teaspoons	dried dill weed
1	envelope	Hidden Valley® Ranch Dip Mix

With sharp knife, cut pork rinds into crouton size pieces. In large plastic bowl with lid, pour oil over pork rinds. Replace lid and shake to coat evenly.

Combine all dry ingredients in small bowl. Sprinkle over oiled pork rinds. Replace lid and shake again to coat evenly. Store in airtight container.

Per 1/6th recipe: 3 g carbs   0 fiber   4 g protein

Food Exchanges: 3 Fat + 1/2 Lean Meat + 1 Starch

Chicken and Watercress Salad

Serves 4

1	teaspoon	dried oregano
1/2	teaspoon	coriander
1/2	teaspoon	ground cumin
1/4	teaspoon	salt
4		chicken breast halves without skin
2	cups	watercress

Preheat broiler and set 6 inches from heat. Combine oregano, coriander, cumin and salt. Rub chicken with mixture. Broil chicken for 4-5 minutes per side or until juices run clear. Let cool. Slice diagonally in 1/2 inch strips and place in bowl with watercress.

2	teaspoons	red wine vinegar
2	teaspoons	oil
1/4	teaspoon	coriander
1/4	teaspoon	dried cumin
1/4	teaspoon	dried oregano
1/4	teaspoon	salt
1		garlic clove -- minced
3/4	cup	tomato -- chopped

Whisk together vinegar, oil, coriander, cumin, oregano and salt. Whisk in the tomato and garlic. Pour dressing over chicken and watercress and toss.

Per 1/4th recipe: 3 g carbs   1 g fiber   28 g protein

Food Exchanges: 1/2 Fat + 4 Lean Meat + 1/2 Vegetable

Cucumber Slices
Serves 6

1-1/2	cups	cucumbers -- thinly sliced
1/4	cup	onion -- sliced
1/4	cup	green pepper -- chopped
1	tablespoon	salt
		water -- to cover
1/4	cup	vinegar
1/2	cup	granular sugar substitute — see page 21
1/4	teaspoon	celery seed

Place cucumbers, onions, peppers and salt in medium mixing bowl. Cover with water and chill for 2 hours.

Mix vinegar, sugar substitute and celery seed thoroughly. Drain water from cucumber mixture and rinse well. Pour dressing over cucumbers. Chill before serving.

Per 1/6th recipe: 2 g carbs 0 g fiber 0 g protein

Food Exchanges: 1/2 Vegetable

Green Bean Salad
with Sunflower Seeds
Serves 4

1	pound	green beans -- fresh
2	tablespoons	sunflower seeds
1	tablespoon	oil
1		garlic clove -- pressed
4	teaspoons	tarragon vinegar
1	cup	spinach leaves -- torn
4		scallions -- chopped

Steam green beans 3-4 minutes or just until tender crisp. Cook sunflower seeds with oil in skillet over medium heat just until golden brown. Remove from heat. Add garlic to skillet and stir well. When seeds and garlic have cooled, add vinegar. Toss green beans with sunflower mixture. Chill. Serve over spinach leaves. Sprinkle with scallions.

Per 1/4th recipe: 10 g carbs   4 g fiber   3 g protein

Food Exchanges: 1 Fat + 1-1/2 Vegetable

Green Bean Salad
with Walnut Dressing
Serves 4

3/4	pound	green beans -- fresh
1/2	cup	walnuts -- chopped
3	tablespoons	rice vinegar
1-1/2	teaspoons	dried dill weed
1/4	teaspoon	Dijon mustard
1	tablespoon	sweet red pepper -- minced

Steam green beans 3-4 minutes or just until tender crisp. Mix walnuts, vinegar, dill and mustard in blender on low speed until smooth, scraping sides frequently. Toss beans with mixture. Sprinkle with peppers. Chill before serving.

Per 1/4th recipe: 9 g carbs   3 g fiber   3 g protein

Food Exchanges: 1-1/2 Fat + 1 Vegetable

Tuna and Nut Salad
Serves 4

12	ounces	canned tuna in water -- drained
1/2	cup	celery -- chopped
1/4	cup	walnuts -- chopped
1/2	cup	Hellman's® mayonnaise
1	tablespoon	dried dill weed
1	teaspoon	dried minced onion flakes
		salt -- to taste
		pepper -- to taste

Combine all ingredients in a small bowl. Mix well.

Per 1/4th recipe: 2 g carbs   1 g fiber   23.g protein

Food Exchanges: 2-1/2 Fat + 3 Lean Meat

"Potato" Salad
Serves 4

3	cups	cauliflower florets
2		eggs — hard-boiled
1	cup	celery -- chopped
1/2	cup	onion -- chopped
1/2	cup	Hellman's® mayonnaise
1/4	teaspoon	prepared mustard
1	packet	sugar substitute — see page 21
		salt -- to taste
		pepper -- to taste

Steam cauliflower until tender but not too soft. Let cool. Chop hard boiled eggs.

Toss cauliflower, eggs, celery and onion. Blend mayonnaise, mustard, sugar substitute, salt and pepper. Pour over cauliflower mixture, stirring until evenly coated.

Per 1/4th recipe: 7 g carbs   3 g fiber   5 g protein

Food Exchanges: 2 Fat + 1/2 Lean Meat + 1 Vegetable

Spinach Salad
with Mustard Dressing

Serves 4

3		eggs, hard-boiled
1-1/2	teaspoons	prepared mustard
3	tablespoons	cider vinegar
3	tablespoons	granular sugar substitute — see page 21
4	cups	spinach leaves -- torn
1/3	cup	bacon drippings -- warmed
2		scallions -- chopped

Separate hard boiled eggs into whites and yolks. Chop the whites. Mix the yolks with mustard, vinegar and sugar substitute until smooth. Combine the spinach leaves and egg dressing in medium bowl. Add warm bacon drippings and toss. Sprinkle chopped egg whites, bacon and scallions over salad.

Per 1/4th recipe: 4 g carbs   1 g fiber   5 g protein

Food Exchanges: 4 Fat + 1/2 Lean Meat + 1/2 Vegetable

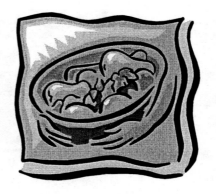

VEGETABLES

Bacon Fried Sauerkraut
Baked Spinach
Batter for Deep Frying Vegetables
Creamed Spinach
Brussel Sprouts with Pecan Butter
Fried "Potatoes"
Savory Green Beans
Hashed Brown Zucchini
Spanish "Rice"
Spinach Delight
Tangy Mustard Cauliflower
Whipped "Potatoes"

Fast & Easy Tips

- Stock up on frozen and canned vegetables.

- Learn to can your own green beans. You do the work once a year and then simply reheat.

- Vegetables fried in butter and seasoned with SPIKE® always work in my house.

- "No Sugar Added" simply means no table sugar added. Be sure to check the ingredients list for dextrose, fructose, sucrose, sorbitol, corn syrup or any other hidden carbs.

- Slice mushrooms with an egg slicing gizmo.

- Use only one third the amount of fresh herbs when substituting dried herbs.

Bacon Fried Sauerkraut
Serves 4

1	pound	bacon -- fried and drained
14	ounces	canned sauerkraut -- drained
1/2	cup	onion -- chopped
3	tablespoons	bacon drippings

Fry bacon, drain, crumble and set aside. Save drippings. Rinse and drain sauerkraut. Fry onions in bacon drippings until brown. Add sauerkraut and bacon. Continue to fry until brown.

Per 1/4th recipe::   7 g carbs   3 g fiber   36 g protein

Food Exchanges: 10 Fat + 4-1/2 Lean Meat + 1 Vegetable

Baked Spinach
Serves 4

20	ounces	frozen chopped spinach -- thawed & drained
1/2	cup	unsalted butter
1	envelope	Kroger® Onion Soup Mix
8	ounces	cream cheese -- softened

Melt butter in frying pan. Add spinach, breaking up while stirring. Cook until heated thoroughly. Remove from heat. Add soup mix and cream cheese. Place in casserole dish.

Bake at 300° for 45 minutes.

Per 1/4th recipe: 11 g carbs   4 g fiber   9 g protein

Food Exchanges: 8 Fat + 1/2 Lean Meat + 1/2 Vegetable + 1/2 Starch

Batter for Deep Frying Vegetables
Serves 6

1		egg -- beaten
1/3	cup	half & half
1/2	cup	Fearn® Soya Powder
		salt -- to taste
		pepper -- to taste

In small bowl, beat egg with half & half. Place soya powder in a zip-lock plastic bag. Dip selected vegetables in egg mixture then place in plastic bag and shake to coat evenly with powder. Drop coated vegetables in pre-heated oil in deep fryer. Coating will fry quickly. Remove and salt and pepper to taste.

Per 1/6th recipe: 3 g carbs   1 g fiber   5 g protein

Food Exchanges: 1/2 Fat + 1/2 Lean Meat

Creamed Spinach
Serves 4

1/2	cup	onion -- chopped fine
2	tablespoons	unsalted butter
20	ounces	frozen chopped spinach -- thawed & drained
8	ounces	cream cheese -- softened
3/4	cup	Parmesan cheese

Sauté onions in butter until tender. Add remaining ingredients. Mix well. Place mixture in casserole.

Bake at 350° for 10 minutes or until warm.

Per 1/4th recipe: 9 g carbs   5 g fiber   15 g protein

Food Exchanges: 5 Fat + 1-1/2 Lean Meat + 1-1/2 Vegetables

Brussel Sprouts
with Pecan Butter

Serves 8

1	quart	water
1	teaspoon	salt
1-1/2	pounds	Brussel sprouts -- fresh
2	cups	Swanson's® Fat-Free Chicken Broth
2	tablespoons	onion -- chopped
1/2	teaspoon	salt
1/2	cup	pecans -- chopped
1/2	cup	unsalted butter

Wash Brussel sprouts. Soak in water (with 1 teaspoon salt added) for 20 minutes. Drain and rinse thoroughly.

In large pan, add chicken broth, Brussel sprouts, onion and remaining salt. Boil for 5 minutes. Reduce heat, cover and cook for an additional 10 minutes or until tender. Drain.

Sauté pecans in butter in separate pan for 3 minutes. Add Brussel sprouts and toss lightly.

Per 1/8th recipe: 9 g carbs   3 g fiber   4 g protein

Food Exchanges: 3 Fat + 1-1/2 Vegetable

Fried "Potatoes"
Serves 4

10	slices	bacon -- fried and drained
3	cups	cauliflower -- sliced
1/2	cup	onion -- sliced
1	teaspoon	garlic powder
6	tablespoons	bacon drippings

Reserve bacon drippings. Crumble bacon and set aside. Add cauliflower and onions in drippings until tender. Add garlic powder. Add crumbled bacon and mix thoroughly.

Variations: Add green pepper, broccoli, eggs, mushrooms, Tabasco, cheese topping.

Per 1/4th recipe:	6 g carbs	2 g fiber	7 g protein

Food Exchanges:	5 Fat + 1/2 Lean Meat + 1 Vegetable

Savory Green Beans
Serves 6

3	cups	green beans -- fresh
1/2	envelope	Kroger® Onion Soup Mix
3/4	cup	hot water
2	tablespoons	unsalted butter
2	tablespoons	Parmesan cheese

Mix beans, soup mix and water in microwave-able bowl. Cover tightly and microwave on high for 5 minutes. Stir and replace cover. Microwave additional 6-9 minutes or until beans are tender. Drain. Stir in butter and sprinkle with cheese.

Per 1/6th recipe:	5 g carbs	2 g fiber	2 g protein

Food Exchanges:	1 Fat + 1 Vegetable

Hashed Brown Zucchini
Serves 6

1-1/2	pounds	zucchini -- shredded
1/2	teaspoon	salt
2		eggs
6	tablespoons	Parmesan cheese
1	clove	garlic -- minced
1/4	cup	unsalted butter

Coarsely shred zucchini (should make about 4 cups). Add salt. Let stand for 15 minutes, using hands to squeeze out moisture. Stir in eggs, cheese and garlic. Melt 2 tablespoons of butter in frying pan over medium-high heat.

Make patties out of the zucchini mixture. Fry patties about 6 minutes on each side or until golden. Continue adding butter and frying patties until mixture is gone. Serve warm.

Per 1/6th recipe: 4 g carbs   1 g fiber   5 g protein

Food Exchanges: 2 Fat + 1/2 Lean Meat + 1/2 Vegetable

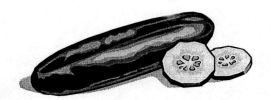

Spanish "Rice"

Serves 4

3	cups	cauliflower florets
1	cup	tomato juice
2	teaspoons	dried minced onion flakes
	dash	garlic powder
1/2	teaspoon	chili powder
1/2	cup	green pepper -- chopped
1/4	cup	Parmesan cheese
1	packet	sugar sweetener — see page 21

Cook cauliflower until tender. Break up with fork until texture resembles rice. In separate pan, combine remaining ingredients and cook until peppers are tender. Pour sauce over cauliflower "rice" and mix well.

Place in small baking dish. Sprinkle cheese on top. Cook at 300° for 15-20 minutes or until bubbly.

Per 1/4th recipe: 9 g carbs   3 g fiber   4 g protein

Food Exchanges: 1/2 Lean Meat + 1-1/2 Vegetable

Spinach Delight
Serves 8

30	ounces	frozen chopped spinach -- thawed & drained
16	ounces	cottage cheese, small curd
2	cups	cheddar cheese -- shredded
3		eggs -- beaten
3	tablespoons	Fearn® Soya Powder
6		scallions -- chopped
2		garlic cloves -- minced
		salt -- to taste
		pepper -- to taste

Thaw spinach and squeeze out the liquid. Mix all ingredients in mixing bowl. Place in 9x13" glass baking dish.

Bake at 325° for 45 minutes.

Per 1/8th recipe: 9 g carbs   4 g fiber   21 g protein

Food Exchanges: 1-1/2 Fat + 2-1/2 Lean Meat + 1 Vegetable

Tangy Mustard Cauliflower

Serves 6

3	cups	cauliflower florets — see page 26
2	tablespoons	water
1/2	cup	Hellman's® mayonnaise
1	teaspoon	prepared mustard
1	teaspoon	dried minced onion flakes
1/2	cup	cheddar cheese – shredded

Place cauliflower in casserole dish. Add water and cover. Microwave on high for 8-9 minutes or until tender.

Combine the mayonnaise, mustard and onion. Mix well. Spoon over cauliflower. Sprinkle with cheese. Microwave for 1-2 minutes more to heat the topping and melt the cheese. Let stand for 2 minutes before serving.

Per 1/6th recipe: 3 g carbs   1 g fiber   4 g protein

Food Exchanges: 1-1/2 Fat + 1/2 Lean Meat + 1/2 Vegetable

Whipped "Potatoes"
Serves 4

3	cups	cauliflower florets — see page 26
8	ounces	cream cheese -- softened
8	ounces	sour cream
2	tablespoons	half & half
1/4	cup	unsalted butter
		salt -- to taste
		pepper -- to taste

Steam cauliflower until tender, puree with butter and half & half. In separate bowl, mix sour cream and cream cheese. Add cauliflower and mix well. Place mixture in baking dish.

Bake at 350° only until brown on top.

Per 1/4th recipe: 8 g carbs   2 g fiber   8 g protein

Food Exchanges: 8-1/2 Fat + 1/2 Lean Meat + 1/2 Vegetable

Favorite Recipes

ENTREES

Breading for Frying Meat
Broccoli and Cheese Soufflé
Broccoli Quiche
Broccoli Romano Soufflé
Cabbage Casserole
Cajun Shrimp
Cheeseburger Quiche
Chicken a la King
Chicken Alfredo
Chicken and Dressing
Chicken Soufflé
Chili Cheese Puff
Eggplant Parmesan
Grilled Tuna Teriyaki
Ham and Asparagus Rolls with Cheese Sauce
Hamburger Biscuit Bake
Meatballs
Meatloaf
No-Crust Spinach Pie
Peppered Chicken with Mustard Sauce
Pizza with Hamburger Crust
Pork Chops – Herb Marinade
Pork Chops – Sage Marinade
Salmon Patties
Quiche Lorraine
Spinach Quiche
Shrimp Alfredo
Shrimp and Broccoli Stir-Fry
Shrimp Foo Young
Stuffed Chicken
Taco Casserole
Vegetable Pie

Fast & Easy Tips

- Stock up on easy to use items such as canned tuna, chicken, chicken broth, salmon, mushrooms, Five Brothers® Alfredo Sauce.

- Look for individually frozen chicken breasts in your freezer section.

- Keep a few protein drinks on hand - great when you're in a hurry but need to eat.

- Eating out for dinner? Look for Caesar's salad with grilled chicken, any unbreaded meats, steamed vegetables, cheeseburgers (don't eat the bun), steak, etc. You can be choosy on a buffet.

- The best steak sauce ever invented is melted butter. All the "high end" restaurants use it.

Breading for Frying Meat

Serves 4

3		egg whites
1/3	cup	whipping cream
1-1/2	cups	pork rinds -- crushed
	dash	dried thyme
	dash	ground sage
	dash	dried rosemary
	dash	dry mustard
	dash	dried tarragon

Whisk egg whites with whipping cream. Place crushed pork rinds on a flat dish. Dip selected meat in egg mixture then coat evenly with pork rinds. Cook meat as normal.

Per 1/4th recipe: 1 g carbs   0 g fiber   30 g protein

Food Exchanges: 8 Fat + 4 Lean Meat

Broccoli and Cheese Soufflé
Serves 4

3	cups	broccoli florets
4		eggs -- separated
1	cup	feta cheese -- crumbled
1/4	teaspoon	coriander
1/4	teaspoon	dried oregano
	dash	ground nutmeg

Drop broccoli in boiling water for about 3 minutes, rinse with cold water and chop. Mix broccoli and egg yolks in blender on medium until smooth. Add feta cheese, coriander, oregano and nutmeg to blender. Mix again until smooth. Scrape sides frequently. Pour mixture into mixing bowl. In separate bowl, beat egg whites until stiff peaks form. Gently stir 1/4 of egg whites into broccoli mixture. Then fold in remainder. Pour into greased 2-quart soufflé dish.

Bake at 325° for 30-35 minutes.

Per 1/4th recipe:	5 g carbs	2 g fiber	12 g protein

Food Exchanges:	1-1/2 Fat + 1-1/2 Lean Meat + 1/2 Vegetable

Broccoli Quiche
Serves 6

4		eggs -- beaten
1	cup	half & half
1/2	teaspoon	salt
9	ounces	frozen chopped broccoli -- thawed & drained
1/4	cup	onion -- chopped
1/2	cup	cheddar cheese -- shredded
1/2	cup	Swiss cheese -- shredded
1/4	cup	Parmesan cheese

Combine eggs, half & half and salt. Mix well. Place broccoli and onions on bottom of well greased 9 inch pie pan. Combine the cheeses and sprinkle over the vegetables. Pour the egg mixture over the cheeses.

Bake at 350° for 40 minutes. Let stand for 10 minutes before slicing.

Per 1/6th recipe: 5 g carbs   1 g fiber   13 g protein

Food Exchanges: 2 Fat + 1-1/2 Lean Meat + 1/2 Vegetable

Broccoli Romano Soufflé
Serves 4

2-1/2	cups	broccoli florets
1	cup	spinach leaves -- torn
2		egg yolks
1/3	cup	Romano cheese -- grated
	dash	ground nutmeg
4		egg whites
1/4	cup	Parmesan cheese -- grated

Drop broccoli in boiling water for about 3 minutes, rinse with cold water and chop. Mix broccoli, spinach and egg yolks in blender on medium until smooth. Scrape sides frequently. Pour mixture into mixing bowl and stir in Romano cheese and nutmeg. In separate bowl, beat egg whites until stiff peaks form. Gently stir in 1/4 of egg whites into broccoli mixture. Then fold in remainder.

Sprinkle Parmesan cheese inside greased 2-quart soufflé dish, coating all sides. Pour mixture into dish.

Bake at 325° for 25-30 minutes.

Per 1/4th recipe:	4 g carbs	2 g fiber	11 g protein

Food Exchanges:	1/2 Fat + 1-1/2 Lean Meat + 1/2 Vegetable

Cabbage Casserole

Serves 4

14	ounces	Hillshire Farm® Beef Smoked Sausage
6	cups	cabbage
1/4	cup	oil
1		egg -- beaten
1/4	cup	onion -- chopped
		salt -- to taste
		pepper -- to taste

Slice sausage into 1/2 inch pieces. In a large skillet, fry sausage on medium-low heat. Chop cabbage into large chunks and pull apart. Add cabbage to sausage and start cooking. (Cabbage will cook down.) Add oil if necessary to keep cabbage from sticking. Add chopped onions and egg. Salt and pepper heavily. Cook for about 30 minutes or until cabbage reaches desired tenderness. Drain before serving.

Per 1/4th recipe: 10 g carbs   3 g fiber   16 g protein

Food Exchanges: 8 Fat + 1 Lean Meat + 1-1/2 Vegetable

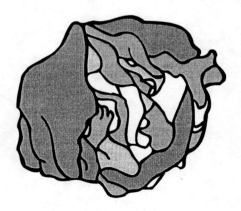

Cajun Shrimp

Serves 4

1	quart	water
2/3	cup	salt
1	teaspoon	black pepper
2	teaspoons	garlic powder
3/4	teaspoon	dried minced onion powder
1/4	teaspoon	ground nutmeg
2	teaspoons	dried parsley
4	teaspoons	cayenne pepper
2	teaspoons	chili powder
2	pounds	shrimp
1/2		lemon

Bring water to boil and add seasonings. Remove from stove and cool in refrigerator. Once cooled, add shrimp and lemon. Put back in refrigerator and leave overnight. When ready to eat, remove shrimp from water. Bring liquid to boil, add shrimp and boil for 5 minutes. Remove from heat and let sit 5 minutes. Drain shrimp and spread on cookie sheet to cool.

Per 1/4th recipe:	6 g carbs	1 fiber	47 g protein

Food Exchanges:	6-1/2 Lean Meat

Cheeseburger Quiche
Serves 4

1/2	pound	ground beef
1/3	cup	onion -- chopped
2		eggs
1/2	cup	Hellman's® mayonnaise
1/2	cup	half & half
1-1/2	cups	cheddar cheese -- shredded
4	ounces	canned mushrooms -- drained
		salt -- to taste
		pepper -- to taste

Brown ground beef and onion. Drain. In separate bowl, beat eggs. Add remaining ingredients to eggs. Add beef mixture. Mix well. Pour into pie pan.

Bake at 350° for 45 minutes. Let stand for 10 minutes before cutting.

Per 1/4th recipe: 5 g carbs   1 g fiber   25 g protein

Food Exchanges: 7 Fat + 3 Lean Meat + 1/2 Vegetable

Chicken á la King
Serves 4

4		chicken breast without skin -- diced
1	tablespoon	oil
1/4	cup	unsalted butter
1/4	cup	Fearn® Soya Powder
1/2	teaspoon	salt
1	cup	whipping cream
1	cup	Swanson's® Fat-Free Chicken Broth
1/2	cup	mushrooms
2	ounces	pimientos -- chopped
4	slices	Healthy Life® 100% Whole Wheat Bread -- toasted

Brown chicken lightly in oil. Add remaining ingredients to skillet. Simmer until excess whipping cream and broth cooks down and chicken is tender.

Serve over toasted Healthy Life® bread.

Per serving:	10 g carbs	3 g fiber	32 g protein

Food Exchanges: 7 Fat + 4 Lean Meat + 1/2 Starch

Chicken Alfredo

Serves 6

6		chicken breasts without skin
4	ounces	canned mushrooms
1/4	cup	onion -- chopped
1/2	cup	celery -- chopped
1/4	cup	oil
1/2	jar	Five Brothers® Alfredo Sauce
1/4	cup	fresh parsley -- chopped

Sauté chicken in oil for 5 minutes on each side or until slightly brown. Remove chicken from oil and place in shallow baking dish.

Sauté mushrooms, onions and celery in remaining oil. Add Alfredo sauce and parsley and mix well. Pour sauce over chicken.

Bake at 375° for 10 minutes or until heated thoroughly.

Per 1/6th recipe: 3 g carbs   1 g fiber   29 g protein

Food Exchanges: 2-1/2 Fat + 4 Lean Meat + 1/2 Vegetable

Chicken and Dressing
Serves 1

1		chicken bouillon cube
1/2	cup	water
1/2	cup	celery -- chopped
1/2	cup	mushrooms
1	teaspoon	poultry seasoning
1/4	teaspoon	sage
1	tablespoon	dried minced onion flakes
4	ounces	canned chicken -- drained
1	slice	Healthy Life® 100% Whole Wheat Bread -- cubed

Dissolve bouillon in water in small sauce pan over medium heat. Add celery, mushrooms and seasonings. Cook until tender. Layer chicken in bottom of greased baking dish. Layer bread cubes over chicken. Pour celery mixture over layers.

Bake at 400° for 45 minutes.

Per recipe:	15 g carbs	4 g fiber	27 g protein

Food Exchanges:	3-1/2 Lean Meat + 1 Starch + 1/2 Vegetable

Chicken Soufflé

Serves 4

4		chicken breasts without skin
2	tablespoons	unsalted butter
1	teaspoon	dried thyme
2/3	cup	Hellman's® mayonnaise
1/3	cup	sour cream
1/3	cup	Parmesan cheese

Sauté chicken in butter for 5 minutes on each side or until slightly brown. Arrange chicken in shallow baking dish. Sprinkle chicken with thyme. Combine remaining ingredient in separate bowl. Spoon mixture over chicken.

Bake at 350° for about 40 minutes or until golden brown.

Per 1/4th recipe: 1 g carbs   0 g fiber   31 g protein

Food Exchanges: 4-1/2 Fat + 4 Lean Meat

Chili Cheese Puff

Serves 6

5		eggs
1/2	teaspoon	baking powder
1/4	cup	Fearn® Soya Powder
1/4	teaspoon	salt
1	cup	cottage cheese, small curd
1/2	pound	Monterey jack cheese -- shredded
1/4	cup	unsalted butter -- melted
1/3	cup	green chilies
1	teaspoon	xanthan gum

Beat eggs until light and lemon colored. Add baking powder, soy powder, salt, cottage cheese, shredded cheese and melted butter. Mix well. Add chilies and xanthan gum. Pour mixture into well greased 8 or 9 inch baking dish.

Bake at 350° for 50 minutes or until lightly browned and the center is firm.

Per 1/6th recipe:	5 g carbs	1 g fiber	21 g protein

Food Exchanges:	3-1/2 Fat + 3 Lean Meat

Eggplant Parmesan

Serves 4

1		medium eggplant
2	slices	Healthy Life® 100% Whole Wheat Bread -- toasted & crumbled
1/2	cup	Parmesan cheese
1		egg
1	tablespoon	water
1	tablespoon	oil
8	ounces	tomato sauce
1-1/2	cups	mozzarella cheese -- shredded

Peel and slice eggplant crosswise into 1/2 inch thick slices. Combine bread crumbs and Parmesan cheese in a shallow pan. Mix egg and water in separate bowl. Dip eggplant slices in egg mixture and then coat with bread mixture. Place single layer of slices in well greased shallow baking dish. Drizzle oil over slices.

Bake at 400° for 30 minutes. Remove from oven and pour tomato sauce over eggplant. Sprinkle with cheese. Return to oven and bake for 7-10 minutes or until cheese has melted.

Per 1/4th recipe: 15 g carbs   5 g fiber   17 g protein

Food Exchanges: 2-1/2 Fat + 2 Lean Meat + 1/2 Starch + 2 Vegetable

Grilled Tuna Teriyaki

Serves 4

2	tablespoons	soy sauce
1	tablespoon	rice vinegar
1		garlic clove -- minced
1	teaspoon	ground ginger
4		tuna steaks -- (6 ounces each)
1	tablespoon	oil

Combine soy sauce, rice vinegar, garlic and ginger in shallow pan. Place tuna in marinade and turn to coat both sides. Cover and refrigerate for 30 minutes, turning after 15 minutes.

Preheat broiler and set rack about 6 inches from heat. Pat tuna steaks dry with paper towels. Coat both sides of tuna with oil. Place on broiler pan and broil for 3 minutes per side. Steaks are done when the tuna flakes easily when tested with a fork.

Per steak:	2 g carbs	0 g fiber	40 g protein

Food Exchanges:	1/2 Fat + 5-1/2 Lean Meat

Ham and Asparagus Rolls
with Cheese Sauce
Serves 8

1/4	cup	unsalted butter -- softened
1/4	cup	Fearn® Soya Powder
1	cup	half & half
1	cup	water
1	teaspoon	Worcestershire sauce
1	teaspoon	salt
1/8	teaspoon	pepper
2-1/2	cups	shredded cheddar cheese
1	teaspoon	not/Starch®
24		asparagus spears
8	ounces	ham slices

Combine first 8 ingredients in sauce pan and stir until blended. Sprinkle in not/Starch® until desired thickness – you may not use it all. Wrap three asparagus spears with a ham slice. Use a toothpick to hold together. Place rolls in shallow baking dish. Cover with cheese sauce.

Bake at 350° for 20 minutes.

Per wrap: 5 g carbs   2 g fiber   17 g protein

Food Exchanges: 4 Fat + 2 Lean Meat + 1/2 Vegetable

Hamburger Biscuit Bake
Serves 6

1	pound	ground beef
1/3	cup	onion -- chopped
2	teaspoons	dried parsley
1/4	teaspoon	pepper
1/4	teaspoon	salt
1/4	teaspoon	hot pepper sauce
1	cup	Carbsense® Zero Carb Baking Mix
4	tablespoons	Hellman's® mayonnaise
1/4	cup	half & half
1/4	cup	water
2	teaspoons	baking powder
1	teaspoon	xanthan gum
1/2	teaspoon	baking soda
1	cup	cheddar cheese -- shredded
1/4	cup	Parmesan cheese
2		eggs -- beaten

Brown beef and onion in skillet. Drain. Add cheese, parsley, salt and pepper to beef and onion. Set aside.

Combine remaining ingredients in separate bowl. Mix into soft dough (it will be thick). Place half of biscuit mixture in bottom of greased 8 inch baking dish. Spread meat mixture over dough. Spread remaining dough on top.

Bake at 375° for 12-15 minutes. Do not over cook.

Per 1/6th recipe:	5 g carbs	3 g fiber	32 g protein

Food Exchanges: 5 Fat + 4 Lean Meat + 1/2 Starch

Meatballs
Serves 8

2	pounds	ground beef
2		eggs
1/2	cup	onion -- chopped
2	teaspoons	garlic powder
1	teaspoon	pepper
1	teaspoon	red pepper flakes
2	teaspoons	Italian seasoning
8	ounces	tomato sauce
1/2	teaspoon	garlic powder
1/2	teaspoon	Italian seasoning
1	cup	mozzarella cheese -- shredded

Combine ground beef, eggs, onion, garlic powder, pepper, red pepper and 2 teaspoons of Italian seasoning in medium bowl. Shape mixture into balls about the size of walnuts. Brown meatballs thoroughly in skillet.

Combine remaining ingredients in sauce pan. (Simmer sauce while browning meatballs.) Add meatballs to sauce. Let simmer all day if using crockpot or for at least 1/2 hour in regular pan. Top with cheese before serving.

Per 1/4th recipe: 4 g carbs   1 g fiber   24 g protein

Food Exchanges: 5 Fat + 3-1/2 Lean Meat + 1/2 Vegetable

Meatloaf
Serves 6

1-1/2	pounds	ground beef
2	slices	Healthy Life® 100% Whole Wheat Bread
1/2	cup	half & half
1/3	cup	tomato sauce -- canned
1		egg
1/4	cup	Parmesan cheese
1/3	cup	green pepper -- chopped
		salt -- to taste
		pepper -- to taste

Crumble bread into bowl and pour half & half on it. When bread has soaked up all liquid, add the remaining ingredients. Mix well. Put into casserole dish.

Bake at 350° for 1 hour.

Per 1/6th recipe:	4 g carbs	1 g fiber	22 g protein
Food Exchanges:	5 Fat + 3 Lean Meat		

No-Crust Spinach Pie
Serves 8

1	cup	cottage cheese – small curd
1/4	cup	half & half
3		eggs
1/4	teaspoon	Dijon mustard
1/2	cup	cheddar cheese -- shredded
4		scallions -- chopped
1	teaspoon	oil
4	cups	spinach leaves -- torn
1-1/2	teaspoons	dried dill weed

Mix cottage cheese, half & half, eggs and mustard in blender on medium until smooth. Mix in cheddar cheese. Cook scallions in oil in skillet over low heat. Add spinach leaves and cook until wilted, stirring constantly. Mix in dill.

Spread spinach mixture in bottom of greased 8 inch pie pan. Pour cottage cheese mixture over spinach layer. Sprinkle with nutmeg.

Bake at 350° for 35-40 minutes.

Per 1/8th recipe: 3 g carbs   1 g fiber   9 g protein

Food Exchanges: 1 Fat + 1 Lean Meat

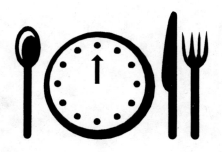

Peppered Chicken
with Mustard Sauce
Serves 4

2	teaspoons	black peppercorns -- crushed
4		chicken breasts without skin
2	teaspoons	oil
1/4	teaspoon	salt
1/4	cup	water
1	cup	Swanson's® Fat-Free Chicken Broth
6		scallions -- chopped
1/3	cup	sour cream
1	teaspoon	not/Starch®
2	teaspoons	Dijon mustard

Press crushed peppercorns into the chicken. Sprinkle with oil and salt. Place chicken in well greased shallow baking dish. Bake at 425° for 15-20 minutes or until juices run clear. Cut each breast diagonally into 1/4 inch slices.

Boil water and scallions in small uncovered sauce pan about 2 minutes until liquid is reduced to 2 tablespoons. Add chicken broth and boil about 2 more minutes until liquid is reduced to 1 cup. Reduce heat to low and add sour cream. Sprinkle in not/Starch® until desired thickness – you may not use it all. Whisk for 1 minute. Stir in mustard. Spoon sauce over sliced chicken breasts.

Per serving:	5 g carbs	2 g fiber	29 g protein

Food Exchanges:	1-1/2 Fat + 4 Lean Meat + 1/2 Vegetable

Pizza with Hamburger Crust

Serves 8

2	pounds	ground beef (or turkey)
2		eggs
1	teaspoon	garlic powder
2	teaspoons	salt
1	teaspoon	pepper
1	teaspoon	Italian seasoning

Mix together all ingredients. Press onto cookie sheet or pizza pan to 1/2 thick.

Bake at 375° for 30 minutes. Pour off fat.

Per 1/8th recipe: 1 g carbs   0 g fiber   20 g protein
(crust only)

Food Exchanges: 4-1/2 Fat + 3 Lean Meat

Variations: Add low-carb topping of your choice:
shredded cheese, peppers, onions, mushrooms, pepperoni, sausage, tomato puree, etc.

After adding toppings, bake at 375° until cheese has melted.

Pork Chops - Herb Marinade
Serves 4

3/4	teaspoon	ground allspice
2		bay leaves -- crushed
1/2	teaspoon	salt
1/2	teaspoon	granular sugar substitute — see page 21
1/4	teaspoon	ground cinnamon
1/4	teaspoon	black pepper
1/4	teaspoons	ground ginger
4		pork chops

Combine all seasonings in a small bowl. Rub mixture into both sides of the pork chops. Wrap in plastic wrap and refrigerate a minimum of 6 hours.

Preheat broiler and set rack about 6 inches from heat. Place pork chops on lightly greased broiler pan and broil for 3-4 minutes per side.

Per pork chop: 5 g carbs   1 g fiber   24 g protein

Food Exchanges: 1 Fat + 3-1/2 Lean Meat + 1/2 Starch

Pork Chops - Sage Marinade
Serves 4

3	tablespoons	oil
2	tablespoons	apple cider
1-1/2	teaspoons	ground sage
1/8	teaspoon	pepper
4		pork chops

Combine oil, apple cider, sage and pepper in plastic food storage bag. Add pork chops, remove excess air, reseal and refrigerate for 30 minutes.

Remove pork chops from bag and cook in skillet over medium heat for 3 minutes per side or until center is no longer pink.

| Per pork chop: | 1 g carbs | 0 g fiber | 23 g protein |

| Food Exchanges: | 3 Fat + 3-1/2 Lean Meat |

Salmon Patties
Serves 4

15	ounces	canned salmon -- drained
3	tablespoons	Carbsense® Zero Carb Baking Mix
1		egg -- beaten
1/4	cup	fresh parsley -- chopped
1	teaspoon	dried dill weed
		salt -- to taste
		pepper -- to taste
1	tablespoon	oil

Mix all ingredients in small mixing bowl. Shape mixture into 4 patties. Fry in oil to desired crispness.

| Per patty: | 1 g carbs | 1 g fiber | 26 g protein |

| Food Exchanges: | 1 Fat + 3 Lean Meat |

Quiche Lorraine
Serves 6

4		eggs -- beaten
1	cup	half & half
1/2	teaspoon	salt
1	cup	Swiss cheese -- shredded
1/4	cup	onion -- chopped
12	pieces	bacon -- cooked and chopped
1/4	cup	Parmesan cheese

Combine eggs, half & half and salt. Mix well. Place bacon and onions on bottom of well greased 9 inch pie pan. Combine the cheeses and sprinkle over the bacon and onions. Pour the egg mixture over the cheeses.

Bake at 350° for 40 minutes. Let stand for 10 minutes before slicing.

Per 1/6th recipe: 3 g carbs   0 g fiber   16 g protein

Food Exchanges: 3 Fat + 2 Lean Meat

Spinach Quiche

Serves 6

4		eggs -- beaten
1	cup	half and half
1/2	teaspoon	salt
9	ounces	frozen chopped spinach -- thawed and drained
1/4	cup	onion -- chopped
1	cup	Swiss cheese -- shredded
1/4	cup	Parmesan cheese

Combine eggs, half & half and salt. Mix well. Place spinach and onions on bottom of well greased 9 inch pie pan. Combine the cheeses and sprinkle over the vegetables. Pour the egg mixture over the cheeses.

Bake at 350° for 40 minutes. Let stand for 10 minutes before slicing.

Per 1/6th recipe: 5 g carbs   1 g fiber   13 g protein

Food Exchanges: 2 Fat + 1-1/2 Lean Meat

Shrimp Alfredo
Serves 6

1-1/2	pounds	shrimp – cooked
1/4	cup	oil
4	ounces	canned mushrooms — drained
1/4	cup	onion -- chopped
1/2	cup	celery -- chopped
1/2	jar	Five Brothers® Alfredo Sauce
1/4	cup	fresh parsley -- chopped

Place shrimp in bottom of shallow baking dish.

Sauté mushrooms, onions and celery in remaining oil. Add Alfredo sauce and parsley and mix well. Pour sauce over shrimp.

Bake at 375° for 10 minutes or until heated thoroughly.

Per 1/6th recipe:	3 g carbs	1 g fiber	25 g protein

Food Exchanges: 2-1/2 Fat + 3-1/2 Lean Meat + 1/2 Vegetable

Shrimp and Broccoli Stir-Fry

Serves 4

1/2	cup	onion -- chopped
2		garlic clove -- sliced
1	tablespoon	oil
3	cups	broccoli florets -- chopped
2	cups	mushrooms -- sliced
1	pound	shrimp -- shelled and deveined
1/2	pound	snow peas
1	tablespoon	soy sauce
2	teaspoons	fresh ginger -- minced

Cut onions in half lengthwise, then slice crosswise into thin half-circles. Add onions and garlic to oil in skillet over medium heat. Stir quickly until translucent. Add broccoli and stir fry until bright green. Add mushrooms and stir fry until they release their liquid. Add shrimp, snow peas, soy sauce and ginger. Stir fry until shrimp are cooked thoroughly and the vegetables are tender-crisp.

Per 1/4th recipe: 9 g carbs   3 g fiber   26 g protein

Food Exchanges: 1/2 Fat + 3 Lean Meat + 1-1/2 Vegetable

Shrimp Foo Young
Serves 4

1	teaspoon	fresh ginger -- minced
6		scallions -- chopped
1/4	cup	celery -- chopped
2	tablespoons	oil
2	cups	bean sprouts
1/4	cup	shrimp -- cooked and chopped
6		eggs -- beaten
2	teaspoons	soy sauce
2	teaspoons	water

Cook ginger, scallions and celery in 1 tablespoon of oil in skillet over medium heat until translucent but still tender-crisp. Mix bean sprouts, cooked shrimp, eggs and cooked vegetables in separate bowl. Heat remaining oil in skillet. Pour 1/4 egg mixture into skillet making total of 4 "pancakes." Cook until golden brown on both sides.

Mix soy sauce and water in bowl. Sprinkle over hot "pancakes" before serving.

Per 1/4th recipe:	6 g carbs	2 g fiber	13 g protein

Food Exchanges:	2 Fat + 1-1/2 Lean Meat + 1 Vegetable

Stuffed Chicken

Serves 4

1	tablespoon	unsalted butter
6		scallions -- chopped
4		mushrooms -- chopped
2		ham center slices -- cubed
1	slice	Healthy Life® 100% Whole Wheat Bread -- cubed
1	tablespoon	Parmesan cheese
2	tablespoons	dried parsley
		salt -- to taste
		pepper -- to taste
4		chicken breasts without skin

Melt butter in skillet. Add scallions, stirring constantly for 1 minute. Add mushrooms, stirring constantly for 2 minutes. Pour mixture into bowl. Add ham, bread crumbs, cheese, parsley, salt and pepper. Mix well and let cool.

Preheat broiler and set rack about 7 inches from heat. using sharp knife, cut a pocket in the thickest part of each chicken breast. Fill each pocket with 1/4 of stuffing mixture. Close opening with toothpick. Place on lightly greased broiler pan and broil for 4-5 minutes per side. Chicken is done when juices run clear.

Per chicken breast:	4 g carbs	1 g fiber	40 g protein

Food Exchanges: 1 Fat + 5-1/2 Lean Meat + 1/2 Vegetable

Taco Casserole

Serves 8

2	pounds	ground beef
1/4	cup	onion -- chopped
1/3	cup	green chili peppers
1/2	cup	green pepper -- chopped
6	teaspoons	taco seasoning mix
8	ounces	Pace® picante sauce
2	cups	cheddar cheese -- shredded

Brown ground beef, onions, chilies and peppers. Drain grease and add taco seasoning. Let simmer for 5 minutes. Add picante sauce and mix well. Continue cooking until warmed thoroughly. Pour mixture into casserole dish and sprinkle with cheese.

Cook at 350° only until cheese melts.

Per 1/8th recipe:	4 g carbs	0 g fiber	26 g protein

Food Exchanges: 6 Fat + 3-1/2 Lean Meat + 1/2 Vegetable

Vegetable Pie
Serves 6

1	cup	broccoli florets -- chopped
1	cup	cauliflower florets -- chopped
2	cups	spinach leaves -- chopped
1/4	cup	onion -- chopped
1/2	cup	green pepper -- chopped
1	cup	cheddar cheese -- shredded
2	tablespoons	oil
2	tablespoons	water
1/2	cup	Carbsense® Zero Carb Baking Mix
4		eggs
1	teaspoon	baking powder
1	teaspoon	garlic salt
1/4	teaspoon	ground nutmeg
1/2	teaspoon	pepper
1	teaspoon	xanthan gum

Drop broccoli and cauliflower in boiling water for about 5 minutes or until almost tender. Drain. Mix broccoli, cauliflower, spinach, onion, green pepper and cheese and put into well greased 10 inch pie pan.

Mix oil, water, soy mix, eggs, baking powder, garlic salt, nutmeg, pepper and xanthan gum in separate bowl. Pour mixture over vegetables.

Bake at 400° for 35 minutes. Let stand 5 minutes before cutting.

Per 1/6th recipe:	6 g carbs	3 g fiber	15 g protein

Food Exchanges: 1 Fat + 1-1/2 Lean Meat + 1/2 Vegetable

Favorite Recipes

DESSERTS

Baked Cheesecake
Banana Nut Snack Cake
Basic Cookie Dough
Blueberry Dessert
Bread Pudding
Brownies
Chocolate Bites
Chocolate Drops
Chocolate Fudge
Jell-O® Delight
Chocolate Kisses
Chocolate Peanut Butter Squares
Chocolate Pie
Chocolate Sauce I
Chocolate Sauce II
Cinnamon Crisps
Frosting
Ice Cream
Pudding
No-Bake Cheesecake
Macadamia Nut Brittle
Peanut Butter Cookies
Pie Crust - Pecan
Pie Pastry
Quick Cookies

Fast & Easy Tips

- Chocolate is a personal thing – experiment with the amount of chocolate & sweetener used in each recipe.

- If you're not using Splenda®, use a combination of sweeteners for better taste. See page 21.

- In a hurry? Whip up some whipping cream with a little sugar substitute and your favorite extract.

- Try sugar free gelatin with whipped cream topping. It's easy.

- Keep some Chocolate Bites or Kisses in the refrigerator for any sudden urges.

- not/Sugar® is not necessary for sweetened recipes but vastly improves the texture.

- Be aware that whipping cream, cream cheese and artificial sweeteners only have 0 carbs for very small servings. See page 7 for the correct numbers.

Baked Cheesecake

Serves 12

16	ounces	cream cheese -- softened
3/4	cup	granular sugar substitute — see page 21
2	teaspoons	vanilla extract
1	teaspoon	not/Sugar®
2		eggs

Blend cream cheese, sugar substitute, vanilla and not/Sugar®. Add eggs and mix well. Pour into 9" pie pan.

Bake at 350° for 40-45 minutes.

| Per 1/12th recipe: | 2 g carbs | 0 fiber | 4 g protein |

| Food Exchanges: | 2-1/2 Fat + 1/2 Lean Meat |

Variations:

Pecan - Place 1/2 cup pecan halves around edge before baking.
Chocolate Chip - Add 2 TBSP. mini semi-sweet chocolate chips to final mixture before baking.
Peanut Butter - Add 4 TBSP. peanut butter to final mixture before baking.
Pecan Crust - see page 148.
Graham Cracker Crust - Crumble graham cracker lightly over bottom of pan.

Banana Nut Snack Cake
Serves 8

1/2	cup	Carbsense® Zero Carb Baking Mix
3/4	cup	granular sugar substitute — see page 21
2	teaspoons	baking powder
2	teaspoons	not/Sugar®
4		eggs
2	tablespoons	oil
2	tablespoons	water
1	teaspoon	ReaLemon® lemon juice
2	teaspoons	banana extract
1/2	cup	walnuts -- chopped

Combine all dry ingredients separately. Mix the wet ingredients together separately. Blend the wet mixture into the dry mixture. Add nuts. Pour into a well greased 11x7" baking pan.

Bake at 350° for no more than 10-12 minutes.

Per 1/8th recipe:	4 g carbs	2 g fiber	8 g protein

Food Exchanges:	1-1/2 Fat + 1 Lean Meat

Basic Cookie Dough
Serves 24

2/3	cup	unsalted butter -- softened
1	cup	granular sugar substitute — see page 21
1		egg
1	teaspoon	vanilla extract
1	cup	Carbsense® Zero Carb Baking Mix
2	ounces	cream cheese -- softened
1	tablespoon	not/Sugar®
1	tablespoon	whipping cream

Combine all ingredients except whipping cream. Add whipping cream only if needed to correct consistency. Shape dough into 24 walnut-sized balls. Place on well greased cookie sheet. Gently flatten.

Bake at 350° for 8-9 minutes.

Per cookie: 1 g carbs   1 g fiber   3 g protein

Food Exchanges: 1/2 Fat + 1/2 Lean Meat

Variations:
Chocolate Chip - Add 2 TBSP. mini semi-sweet chocolate chips to mixture before shaping.
Chocolate - Add 1 TBSP. unsweetened cocoa and 1/4 cup more sugar substitute.
Nuts - Add 1/4 cup chopped walnuts or pecans.
Snickerdoodles - Sprinkle with cinnamon before baking.

Blueberry Dessert
Serves 6

3		eggs
3	tablespoons	granular sugar substitute — see page 21
1/3	cup	Fearn® Soya Powder
1/2	cup	whipping cream
1/2	cup	water
1/2	teaspoon	almond extract
1/4	teaspoon	salt
1	cup	blueberries

Whisk eggs and sugar substitute in medium bowl. Gradually whisk in soya powder until smooth. Add whipping cream, water, almond extract and salt. Drain liquid from berries. Scatter berries evenly in bottom of 9" pan. Pour batter over berries.

Bake at 375° for 25-30 minutes or until sides are puffed and golden and the center is set. Cool before cutting. (Top with whipped butter or cream.)

Per 1/6th recipe:	6 g carbs	1 g fiber	6 g protein

Food Exchanges: 2 Fat + 1/2 Lean Meat

Bread Pudding

Serves 2

4	slices	Bread I (see recipe, page 45)
2		eggs -- beaten
1/2	cup	half & half
1/2	cup	water
1/4	cup	granular sugar substitute — see page 21
1	teaspoon	vanilla extract
	dash	ground nutmeg
	dash	ground cinnamon

Cut bread into cubes. Place in bottom of small glass baking dish. In separate bowl, beat eggs, half & half and water. Add sugar substitute, cinnamon and nutmeg. Mix well. Pour mixture over bread cubes. Let soak for 15 minutes.

Bake at 350° for 35-40 minutes or until set.

Per 1/2 recipe: 5 g carbs   0 g fiber   17 g protein

Food Exchanges: 3 Fat + 1 Lean Meat + 1 Starch

Brownies
Serves 16

1/2	cup	unsalted butter -- melted
1/3	cup	unsweetened cocoa powder
1	cup	granular sugar substitute — see page 21
1	teaspoon	vanilla extract
1/3	cup	Carbsense® Zero Carb Baking Mix
1	teaspoon	baking powder
1/2	teaspoon	baking soda
1/4	cup	walnuts -- chopped
1	ounce	cream cheese -- softened
2		eggs
1	tablespoon	not/Sugar®

Combine melted butter and cocoa powder. Mix well. Add remaining ingredients. Batter will be thick. Spread into well greased 8″ pan.

Bake at 350° for 20-22 minutes. (Turn pan after first 10 minutes.) Let cool 5 minutes before cutting.

Per 1/16th recipe:	3 g carbs	2 g fiber	3 g protein

Food Exchanges:	1-1/2 Fat + 1/2 Lean Meat

Variations: Vary the amount of unsweetened cocoa and sugar substitute if you like more of a milk chocolate taste.

Chocolate Bites
Serves 12

2	tablespoons	unsalted butter
2	tablespoons	unsweetened cocoa powder
2	tablespoons	whipping cream
1	tablespoon	peanut butter
8	packets	sugar substitute — see page 21

Melt butter with cocoa in microwave. Stir well. Add remaining ingredients. Drop by spoonfuls onto waxed paper and refrigerate.

Per 1/12th recipe:	1 carbs	0 g fiber	1 g protein

Food Exchanges:	1/2 Fat

Chocolate Drops
Serves 24

1	cup	whipping cream
6	ounces	cream cheese -- softened
2	tablespoons	sour cream
1/4	cup	whipping cream
1	small package	instant sugar-free pudding mix -- chocolate

Whip 1 cup of whipping cream in small bowl and set aside. In separate bowl, mix cream cheese, sour cream and remaining whipping cream. Stir in pudding mix and blend well. Fold in whipped cream.

Use a ziploc bag with a corner snipped off to squirt "kisses" onto waxed paper. Place in freezer until solid. Store in refrigerator.

Per 1/24th recipe:	2 carbs	0 g fiber	1 g protein

Food Exchanges:	1-1/2 Fat

Chocolate Fudge
Serves 16

16	ounces	cream cheese -- softened
1	ounce	unsweetened baking chocolate squares -- melted and cooled
3/4	cup	granular sugar substitute — see page 21
1	teaspoon	vanilla extract
1	teaspoon	not/Sugar®
1/2	cup	pecans -- chopped

Beat cream cheese, chocolate, sugar substitute, not/Sugar® and vanilla until smooth in small bowl. Stir in pecans. Pour into 8" square baking pan lined with foil. Cover and chill overnight before cutting.

Per 1/16th recipe:	2 g carbs	1 g fiber	3 g protein

Food Exchanges: 2-1/2 Fat + 1/2 Lean Meat

Jell-O® Delight
Serves 12

2	small packages	sugar-free gelatin mix -- any flavor
4	cups	water
2	cups	whipping cream
1	cup	granular sugar substitute — see page 21
8	ounces	cream cheese -- softened

Prepare gelatin as instructed on package. Cool in refrigerator. Beat whipping cream until stiff. Mix sugar substitute into cream cheese. Add whipping cream to cream cheese mixture. Pour gelatin into this mixture and mix well. Chill until set.

Per 1/12th recipe:	2 g carbs	0 g fiber	2 g protein

Food Exchanges: 4 Fat

Chocolate Kisses
Serves 75

1/4	cup	unsalted butter
3	tablespoons	unsweetened cocoa
1/2	cup	whipping cream
3/4	cup	granular sugar substitute — see page 21
2	teaspoons	vanilla extract
1/3	cup	unsweetened coconut flakes

Melt butter over low heat. Add cocoa and mix well. Slowly add whipping cream. Bring to a boil, stirring frequently. Remove from heat and add sugar substitute and vanilla. Chill until stiff. Remove from refrigerator and whip with mixer until slightly fluffy and lighter in color. Stir in coconut.

Use a ziploc bag with a corner snipped off to squirt "kisses" (75) onto waxed paper. Place in freezer until solid. Store in refrigerator.

Per kiss: 1/2 g carbs   0 g fiber   0 g protein

Food Exchanges: 0

Chocolate Peanut Butter Squares

Serves 16

7	tablespoons	peanut butter
3	ounces	cream cheese -- softened
2	tablespoons	whipping cream
4	packets	sugar substitute — see page 21
3	ounces	unsweetened baking chocolate squares
1/2	cup	unsalted butter
8	tablespoons	whipping cream
1	tablespoon	vanilla extract
18	packets	sugar substitute — see page 21

Mix peanut butter, cream cheese, 2 TBSP. whipping cream and 4 sugar substitute packets well and set aside.

Melt chocolate with butter in microwave. Stir in remaining whipping cream, vanilla and sugar substitute packets. Spread half the chocolate mixture in bottom of well greased 8" pan. Spread peanut butter mixture on chocolate. Pour remaining chocolate on top. (Microwave chocolate mixture slightly if necessary to pour.) Chill before cutting.

Per 1/16th recipe:	5 g carbs	1 g fiber	3 g protein

Food Exchanges:	3-1/2 Fat + 1/2 Lean Meat

Chocolate Pie

Serves 8

2		egg whites
1/8	teaspoon	cream of tartar
1/2	cup	granular sugar substitute — see page 21
1/4	cup	pecans -- finely chopped
1/2	teaspoon	vanilla extract
1	ounce	unsweetened baking chocolate squares
3	tablespoons	water
1	teaspoon	vanilla extract
1	cup	whipping cream
1/2	cup	granular sugar substitute — see page 21

Combine egg whites with cream of tartar in mixing bowl. Beat until foamy. Gradually add sugar substitute, beating until stiff peaks form. Fold in chopped pecans and vanilla. Spoon into lightly greased 8" pie pan, building up 1/2" above edge of pan.

Bake at 300° for 40-45 minutes. Let cool.

Melt chocolate in microwave. Add water, stirring until smooth. Mixture will thicken as it cools. Add vanilla. Whip the cream with the sugar substitute. Fold chocolate into whipped cream. Spoon into crust. Chill before serving.

Per 1/8th recipe:	3 g carbs	1 g fiber	2 g protein
Food Exchanges:	3 Fat		

Chocolate Sauce I
Serves 4

1	cup	ricotta cheese
1/4	cup	unsweetened cocoa powder
1/3	cup	granular sugar substitute — see page 21
1	teaspoon	vanilla extract
1	teaspoon	not/Sugar®
1	tablespoon	half & half

Blend all ingredients well, using half & half to obtain desired consistency.

Per 1/4th recipe:	6 g carbs	2 g fiber	5 g protein

Food Exchanges:	1/2 Fat + 1/2 Lean Meat

Chocolate Sauce II
Serves 8

3/4	cup	whipping cream
3/4	cup	unsweetened cocoa
2	tablespoons	unsalted butter
2	teaspoons	vanilla extract
	dash	salt
3/4	cup	granular sugar substitute — see page 21
1	teaspoon	not/Sugar®

Gradually stir half & half into the cocoa in a small sauce pan. Add butter and cook over medium heat to just simmering, stirring frequently. Stir in vanilla, sugar substitute, salt and not/Sugar®. Cool.

Per 1/8th recipe:	6 g carbs	3 g fiber	2 g protein

Food Exchanges:	2-1/2 Fat + 1/2 Starch

Cinnamon Crisps
Serves 12

12		whole wheat tortillas, La Tortilla Factory®
1/4	cup	oil
1	tablespoon	cinnamon
1/4	cup	granular sugar substitute — see page 21

Cut tortillas into wedges. Heat 1" oil until hot in a heavy skillet. Place tortilla pieces in heated oil and fry on both sides until puffy and lightly browned. Drain on paper towel. Mix cinnamon and sugar substitute in small bowl. Sprinkle on drained tortilla pieces.

Per tortilla:	12 g carbs	9 g fiber	2 g protein

Food Exchanges:	1 Fat + 2 Starch

Frosting
Serves 12

1	package	small instant sugar-free pudding mix-any flavor
1	cup	whipping cream
4	ounces	cream cheese -- softened
1	teaspoon	vanilla extract
4	packets	sugar substitute — see page 21

Mix pudding mix with whipping cream. Stir well. Add remaining ingredients and whisk together until smooth. Mixture should be thick enough to spread.

Per 1/12th recipe:	3 g carbs	0 g fiber	1 g protein

Food Exchanges:	2 Fat + 1/2 Starch

Ice Cream
Serves 6

1	cup	half & half
1-1/2	cups	diet orange soda
2		eggs -- beaten
1	cup	whipping cream
8	packets	sugar substitute — see page 21
1	tablespoon	vanilla extract

Heat the half & half and the orange drink until almost boiling. Add eggs, mix and let cool. Mix the whipping cream, vanilla and sugar substitute together. Add to orange drink mixture. Pour into ice cream freezer. Follow freezer directions.

Per 1/6th recipe:	5 g carbs	0 g fiber	4 g protein

Food Exchanges:	4 Fat + 1/2 Lean Meat

Variations: Try different flavors of diet soda and different extracts.

Macadamia Nut Brittle
Serves 10

1	cup	macadamia nuts -- coarsely chopped
1/3	cup	unsalted butter -- softened
1/2	cup	granular sugar substitute — see page 21
1	tablespoon	light corn syrup -- Karo®
1	teaspoon	not/Sugar®

Mix all ingredients in small pan. Cook over low heat until butter and sugar substitute dissolve. Increase heat and boil until mixture turns golden brown and begins to mass together. Stir constantly for 5 minutes. Pour into 11x7" foil lined pan. Cool before breaking into pieces.

Per 1/10th recipe: 4 g carbs   2 g fiber   1 g protein

Food Exchanges: 3 Fat

Pudding
Serves 6

1	small package	instant sugar-free pudding mix -- any flavor
1	cup	whipping cream
1	cup	water
1	packet	sugar substitute — see page 21

Blend all ingredients together. Continue whipping until desired consistency. Spoon into small bowls. Chill before serving.

Per 1/6th recipe: 5 g carbs   0 g fiber   1 g protein

Food Exchanges: 3 Fat + 1/2 Starch

Variation: If this is too thick, use half & half instead of whipping cream.

No-Bake Cheesecake
Serves 12

1	cup	water
1	envelope	Knox® unflavored gelatin
16	ounces	cream cheese -- softened
3/4	cup	granular sugar substitute — see page 21
1	teaspoon	vanilla extract
2	tablespoons	instant sugar-free pudding mix -- any flavor

Sprinkle gelatin over water. Let stand 2 minutes. Microwave mixture on high for 40 seconds. Stir. Let stand additional 2 minutes. Add cream cheese cubes and stir until softened. Blend well with mixer. Add sugar substitute, vanilla, salt and pudding mix. Pour into 8" pie pan or 12 lined muffin tins. Chill about 2 hours or until firm.

Per 1/12th recipe:	4 g carbs	0 g fiber	5 g protein

Food Exchanges:	2-1/2 Fat + 1/2 Starch

Variations:
Chocolate - Replace pudding mix with 2 ounces melted unsweetened chocolate and add 8 more sugar substitute packets.
Lemon - Replace water with sugar-free lemon-lime soda. Do not add pudding mix.
Pumpkin - Reduce cream cheese to 8 ounces. Reduce water to 1/4 cup. Whip 1 cup whipping cream and add to cream cheese mixture. Add 1/2 cup pumpkin puree, 1 tsp. cinnamon and a dash of nutmeg. Do not add pudding mix.

Peanut Butter Cookies
Serves 24

1	cup	Fifty 50® peanut butter -- chunky
1	cup	granular sugar substitute — see page 21
1		egg
1	teaspoon	baking soda
1	teaspoon	not/Sugar®
1/4	cup	Carbsense® Zero Carb Baking Mix — optional

Mix all ingredients in small bowl. Shape mixture into 24 walnut sized balls. Place on well greased cookie sheet. Gently flatten with hand. Make criss-cross pattern in each cookie with fork dipped in granulated sugar substitute.

Bake at 350° for 8-9 minutes. Let set for 2-3 minutes before handling.

Per cookie:	3 g carbs	1 g fiber	4 g protein

Food Exchanges:	1 Fat + 1/2 Lean Meat

Variation — Omit the soy baking mix for a more delicate texture.

Pie Crust - Pecan
Serves 12

2		egg whites
1/8	teaspoon	cream of tartar
1/2	teaspoon	vanilla extract
1/2	cup	granular sugar substitute — see page 21
1/4	cup	pecan meal -- see page 26

Combine egg whites with cream of tartar in mixing bowl. Beat until foamy. Gradually add sugar substitute, beating until stiff peaks form. Fold in chopped pecans and vanilla. Spoon into lightly greased 8" pie pan, building up 1/2" above edge of pan.

Bake at 300° for 40-45 minutes. Let cool.

Per 1/12th recipe:	2 g carbs	0 g fiber	1 g protein
Food Exchanges:	1/2 Fat		

Pie Pastry
Serves 12

1-1/4	cups	almond flour — see page 26
2	tablespoons	granular sugar substitute — see page 21
4	tablespoons	unsalted butter -- cold
5	tablespoons	ice water

Combine almond flour, sugar substitute and salt in mixing bowl. Cut in butter with pastry cutter until mixture resembles coarse crumbs. Mix in water 1 TBSP. at a time. Mix lightly with a fork until soft dough is formed. Chill until ready to use. Makes pastry for 9" pie pan.

Per 1/12th recipe:	2 g carbs	1 g fiber	2 g protein
Food Exchanges:	1 Fat		

Quick Cookies
Serves 24

3/4	cup	Carbsense® Zero Carb Baking Mix
1	small package	sugar-free pudding mix — any flavor
1	teaspoon	not/Sugar®
1/4	cup	oil
1		egg
4	packets	sugar substitute — see page 21
2	tablespoons	whipping cream
2	tablespoons	water

In small mixing bowl, combine soy baking mix, pudding mix and not/Sugar®. Add oil, egg, sugar substitute, whipping cream and water. Mix well. Shape into 24 walnut size balls. Place on greased cookie sheet. Flatten with palm of hand.

Bake at 350° for 12 minutes.

Per cookie::   2 g carbs   1 g fiber   2 g protein

Food Exchanges: 1/2 Fat

Favorite Recipes

INDEX OF RECIPES

DESSERTS

ENTREES

SALADS

SAUCES

SOUPS

VEGETABLES

#1–"Low Carb Recipes Fast & Easy" *AND/OR*
#2–"More ! Low Carb Recipes Fast & Easy"

ORDER FORM

QTY	PRICE	KY ONLY TAX	SHIPPING (1-2 books)	Book #1 or #2?	TOTAL
____	$15.95	6%	FREE (10-15 day delivery)	_____	_____
____	$15.95	6%	$2.00 (2-3 day delivery)	_____	_____

____ Enclosed is my check/money order for $_____

____ Please charge to my   ☐ VISA or   ☐ Master Card

Card No._____ Exp. Date_____

Name on card _____

Signature _____

Please send cookbook(s) to:

Name _____

Address _____

City _____ State _____ Zip _____

Telephone _____

Please return form to:

Brass Pig, LLC
PO Box 43091
Louisville, KY 40253

1-888-229-9677
Fax 1-502-228-7345

www.LowCarbRecipes.com